The Boy From Long Gully

Australia's Unsung Hero From The Early 1900s Heroic Age Of Antarctic Exploration

Wilson McOrist
Foreword By Tim Jarvis AM, Environmental Explorer And Filmmaker

16pt

Copyright Page from the Original Book

Copyright © Wilson McOrist

First published 2021

This book is copyright. Apart from any fair dealing for the purposes of private study, research, criticism or review as permitted under the Copyright Act, no part may be reproduced, stored in a retrieval system or transmitted in any form or by any means, electronic, mechanical, photocopying, recording or otherwise, without written permission.

All inquiries should be made to the publishers.

Big Sky Publishing Pty Ltd
PO Box 303, Newport, NSW 2106, Australia
Phone: 1300 364 611
Fax: (61 2) 9918 2396
Email: info@bigskypublishing.com.au
Web: www.bigskypublishing.com.au

Cover design and typesetting: Think Productions

A catalogue record for this book is available from the National Library of Australia

TABLE OF CONTENTS

Foreword	i
Preface	vii
Introduction	ix
CHAPTER 1: Shackleton's aspirations	1
CHAPTER 2: Two Petty Officers, a clerk and a padre	16
CHAPTER 3: The boy from Long Gully signs on	49
CHAPTER 4: The voice of Caruso in the Antarctic	73
CHAPTER 5: Man-hauling a sledge and 'hoosh'	104
CHAPTER 6: Ten men stranded	143
CHAPTER 7: Winter at the Cape Evans hut	173
CHAPTER 8: Christmas day on the Great Ice Barrier	200
CHAPTER 9: An ailing padre	229
CHAPTER 10: Facing the 360-mile return trek	247
CHAPTER 11: The blizzard	265
CHAPTER 12: Move, or die like Scott	284
CHAPTER 13: Navigating in white out conditions	303
CHAPTER 14: Waiting, and hoping	321
CHAPTER 15: Scurvy	341
CHAPTER 16: Spartan conditions at the Discovery hut	358
CHAPTER 17: Impatience	376
CHAPTER 18: The return of the Aurora, with Shackleton on board	394
Epilogue on Mackintosh and Hayward	407
Richards the unsung hero	414
Postscript	421
Author Note	424
Sources	427
Back Cover Material	430

TABLE OF CONTENTS

Foreword
Preface   vii
Introduction   ix
CHAPTER 1: Shackleton's departures.   1
CHAPTER 2: Two Petty Officers, a clerk and a padre 16
CHAPTER 3: The boy from Long Gully signs on   49
CHAPTER 4: The voice of Caruso in the Antarctic 72
CHAPTER 5: Man-hauling a sledge and 'horsh'   104
CHAPTER 6: Ten men stranded.   143
CHAPTER 7: Winter at the Cape Evans hut.   173
CHAPTER 8: Christmas day on the Great Ice Barrier 200
CHAPTER 9: An ailing padre   229
CHAPTER 10: Facing the 300-mile return trek   247
CHAPTER 11: The blizzard   265
CHAPTER 12: Move, or die like Scott.   286
CHAPTER 13: Navigating in white out conditions.   303
CHAPTER 14: Waiting and hoping   321
CHAPTER 15: Scurvy.   341
CHAPTER 16: Spartan conditions at the Discovery hut.   358
CHAPTER 17: Ninna lenye   379
CHAPTER 18: The return of the Aurora, with Shackleton on board.   384
Epilogue on Mackintosh and Hayward.   407
Richards the unsung hero.   414
Postscript.   421
Author note.   424
Sources.   427
Back Cover Material.   430

Foreword

There was a critical time in my crossing of South Georgia in 2013, where I was imprisoned in a tent with two companions. Sixty to eighty knot winds raged outside, and hypothermia and frostbite stalked us all. Thirty-six hours into our incarceration I recall the words I wrote in my book *Shackleton's EPIC,* describing our decision to press on: "We surveyed the scene outside. It was still a maelstrom, but the wind gusts had diminished in their severity and the sleet had stopped. "It's now or never," said one of my companions. "Let's make it now".

My experiences give some insight into what young Australian Richard Richards faced in 1916, during the Heroic Age of Antarctic Exploration. Richards, with five (English) companions, was just 10 miles from a food depot on the Great Ice Barrier when a fierce blizzard halted their progress. The blizzard raged without let-up for days and the six men ran out of food, and fuel to even melt snow for a drink.

They knew they were ominously close to where Scott, Wilson and Bowers had died on the Great Ice Barrier a few years earlier, but Richards and two men refused to stay in their tent and die. They decided to brave the blizzard. "We are in a very weak state, but we cannot give in. However, we get underway!"

Then, Richards wrote that it was a "desperate time" that forced he and his two companions out into the blizzard to reach a food depot and return to rescue the three others. In 2007, for me, as I recreated the 1913 survival feat of Douglas Mawson, I searched for a word that described the hardship of surviving on my own in the dreadful conditions he faced. The word that immediately came to mind was 'desperate'.

The story of Richard Richards' heroics in the Antarctic, as a member of a support party for Shackleton, are brought to life in Wilson McOrist's book, *The Boy from Long Gully*. In 1914, Richards joined a support party for Ernest Shackleton, and he became embroiled in one of the greatest stories of endurance in the history of polar exploration. Shackleton was planning to cross the Antarctic continent but needed several food depots to be put down by a support party. Despite many difficulties, Richards and his five English companions completed their given task, all the depots were put in place, but then they had to return to safety, over 360 miles across the Great Ice Barrier. Wilson's book brings to life their little-known survival story, from 100 years ago. It is an unrelenting tale that embodies the will-to-live of Douglas Mawson, the heroics of Ernest Shackleton and the tragedy of Captain Robert Scott.

There are many aspects of Richards' life in the Antarctic that I can relate to.

When we left Elephant Island in our replica *James Caird* – the *Alexandra Shackleton,* it was our Primus stove that brought some relief to our conditions. "Baz had got the Primus going, its glow making those of us on deck feel warmer than the -5°C should have allowed us to". One of Richards' companions wrote of similar feelings: "I write this sitting up in my bag, while the primus is going as an extra luxury", and another: "How cheery the Primus sounds, it seems like coming out of a thick London fog into a drawing room."

On my re-enactment of Shackleton's boat journey, we ate the same rations as used by the early explorers, including 'hoosh', which is pemmican – a mixture of dried beef and fat – usually boiled up with crushed biscuits. To me pemmican was "congealed slop, glistening with globules of fat, a dense dark broth ... slimy lukewarm lard with a pungent aroma that overwhelmed the senses." However, Richards and his companions seemed to enjoy it as a constituent of hoosh. One of them stated: "the biscuit is broken into the hoosh by cracking it up first with our teeth – then the first spoonful gives a delicious glowing tingle right through the body."

And of the angst on entering a frozen sleeping bag: One of Richards colleagues wrote "The warmth from the body now sets up a thaw, you turn and shift position, but all is damp while at this stage ... all our clothes, the top ones, are damp". I too recall that sensation of snatching what little sleep we could whilst drying our clothes and reindeer skin sleeping bags with our body heat on our open boat journey retracing Shackleton's original.

On my Antarctic journey in 1999, on foot and unsupported, I pulled my 225kg sled through the bitter cold, unforgiving terrain and rarefied air of the windswept polar plateau. For 17 days my diary entry simply stated, "the toughest day of my life", each day somehow eclipsing the last for that honour. Richards mentions one day of sledge hauling that was his toughest. It was March 1st of 1916. One incapacitated man was strapped on their sledge and two men were unable to help pulling the sledge as they could hardly walk, because of scurvy. So, it was Richards and two others pulling the sledge, with some help from four dogs. When they went to camp, they found tent poles were missing and they could not put up the tent without them. Richards stood on the sledge and looked back over their track and he could see them some distance away. He went back to pick them up and this walk was 'the hardest damn journey I ever made'.

Richard Richards is an unsung Australian hero. His achievements humble us all, including those of us that have sought to follow in the footsteps of those heroic era explorers many years later. I am confident Wilson McOrist's book will elevate his status and rank Richards alongside Douglas Mawson in any yardstick of famous Australians from the early 1900s 'Heroic Age of Antarctic Exploration'.
Tim Jarvis AM

Preface

Douglas Mawson is Australia's most esteemed explorer of the Antarctic. In addition, his will-to-live portrayed in a 100-mile trek to reach the safety of his base after losing his two companions is legendary.

However, the heroic feats of a young Australian in the 1914-1917 Shackleton expedition go beyond those of Mawson.

The young Australian is Richard Richards.

Unfortunately, Richards name is dwarfed by men like Mawson because discussions about expeditions tend to focus on the leaders. That has meant the contribution of Richards, who was a predominant figure in an Antarctic expedition, has been obscured.

What follows is a true story, an historical narrative that brings to life a little-known survival story from 100 years ago. It is an unrelenting tale that embodies the will-to-live of Douglas Mawson, the heroics of Ernest Shackleton and the tragedy of Captain Robert Scott.

Richard Richards is the boy from Long Gully.

Introduction

The so-called 'Heroic Age of Antarctic Exploration' began with men from a Norwegian ship the *Antarctic* going ashore in 1895. This was the first confirmed landing on the continent of Antarctica. The 'Heroic Age' closed little more than twenty years later, with Ernest Shackleton's Imperial Trans-Antarctic Expedition of 1914-1917.

The exploits of just four men, Scott, Amundsen, Shackleton and Mawson usually dominate any analysis of this 'Heroic Age'.

Robert Falcon Scott is the most famous of British Antarctic polar explorers. On his first expedition to the Antarctic, the British National Antarctic (*Discovery*) Expedition of 19011904, Scott wintered his ship at McMurdo Sound in the Ross Sea. Before winter set in the party constructed a hut on a rocky peninsula designated Hut Point, which was used mainly as a storeroom and a shelter. The men lived on board the ship, which was frozen into the sea-ice.

A feature of the *Discovery* Expedition was a southern journey by Scott, Edward Wilson and Ernest Shackleton onto the Great Ice Barrier. The method used by Scott (and later southern bound journey teams) was to first lay a series of food and fuel depots out to the south so the final southbound party would not have to carry supplies for the whole journey.

On this first journey southward in 1902 Scott and his two companions reached the 'furthest south' location at that time, by over 200 miles. This was seen by the press and the public as 'a most heroic effort'. (The Daily Telegraph, Sydney, NSW, Monday 4 Apr 1904.)

However, Scott is primarily known for his second expedition, the *Terra Nova* Expedition. In 1910 he again led a party to the Antarctic and this time a substantial hut was built at Cape Evans in McMurdo Sound, 13 miles to the north of Hut Point. Scott and four others reached the South Pole on January 17, 1912 only to find the black flag of Norway – Roald Amundsen had beaten them by 30 days.

Scott and his four men die tragically as they attempt to return from the pole. 'The late Captain Scott. Strong leader and typical Englishman. A modest hero.', wrote the Daily Telegraph, Sydney, NSW, Wednesday 12 Feb 1913. Scott is often celebrated as the leading hero of Antarctic exploration; because he paid the greatest prize, his death.

Roald Amundsen was a Norwegian explorer, of polar regions to the north and the south. From 1903 to 1906 he led the first expedition through the Northwest Passage by sea. Then, in 1911, he went to the Antarctic, in a race to the South Pole against Scott. He made a premature start but when severe difficulties arose because of the weather, he had the ability to assess his party's situation dispassionately and decide to go back and wait for better weather. He wrote: 'To risk men and animals by continuing stubbornly once we have set off, is something I couldn't consider'. He took eight companions to the South Pole, the first men to reach there, and brought all his men home safely. The brilliance of his achievement to be first to the South Pole places

Amundsen in the foremost rank of Antarctic explorers of the 'Heroic Age'.

The Irishman Ernest Shackleton was with Scott in 1902, but his most heroic exploits relate to two later expeditions, where he was the leader. On the first expedition of Shackleton's, the *Nimrod* Expedition of 1907-09, he hoped to reach the South Pole. Shackleton thought the pole might be located on the Great Ice Barrier which he described 'as level as a billiard table, with no sign of any undulation or rise', however as his party went further south they saw a mountain range to the west slowly curving to cut across their path. Shackleton hoped he might 'find some strait' that would enable his party to go through the mountain range and further southward. The mountains were clear of any snow, with vertical sides and 'not less than 8000 to 9000ft in height'. They came up to a reddish coloured hill in the range, about 3000 feet high, which they named Mount Hope. Shackleton later wrote about the view from its summit: 'there burst upon our view an open road to the south, for there stretched before us a great glacier running almost south and north'; later to be named the Beardmore Glacier. The glacier would be the route towards the South Pole for Shackleton, (and it was for Scott on his final expedition). He and his three companions were within 100 miles of the South Pole when Shackleton made the decision to turn back. They survived the return trek to McMurdo Sound because food depots had been put down for them by a support party. Shackleton returned to Britain a hero. It was reported he said to his wife, *"Better a live donkey than a dead lion."*

Shackleton is most famous for his next expedition, the Trans-Antarctic expedition of 1914-1917. He had two parties of men: his party that would trek across the Antarctic continent, and a Ross Sea support party on the other side of the continent. The support party would put down food depots for the final 360 miles of his trek, between Mount Hope at the foot of the Beardmore Glacier and huts at McMurdo Sound. The food depots were never needed. Shackleton's ship was crushed in the ice before he even landed, and he took all his men to Elephant Island in small boats. Then he and four of the men sailed a boat across the Southern Ocean to South Georgia, where he and two of these men walked across South Georgia to reach a whaling station. Shackleton brought all his men from the *Endurance* home safely. His leadership and heroism from this expedition is still lauded today.

Australians in the 'Heroic Age'

Douglas Mawson is the most prominent figure with Australia's involvement in the 'Heroic Age of the Antarctic'. He was born in England in 1882 and he came to Australia with his parents when he was only two years old. He joined Shackleton's 1907-1909 *Nimrod* expedition and he was in the first party of men to climb Mount Erebus. Then he and two others reached the South Magnetic Pole in an epic journey of courage and endurance journey of four months.

Mawson then launched his own Australasian Antarctic Expedition, which sailed in December 1911. Three scientific bases were established: one at Macquarie Island, and two others in the Antarctic, at Commonwealth Bay and on the Shackleton Ice Shelf. Several land expeditions explored virgin land and conducted major scientific investigations. Mawson was a scientist, but he is remembered more for an expedition in 1912, where he loses his two companions. One falls into a deep crevasse with most of their dogs and food, and the other dies on the way back to base. Mawson's tale of the loss of his companions and his extraordinary fight to survive as he makes his way back alone is one of the most gripping of tales in Antarctic history.

Apart from Mawson, there are other Australians who were in the Antarctic during this 'Heroic Age'.

Carsten Borchgrevink was born and grew up in Norway but as a young man he worked in Australia. In 1894 he signed up for Norwegian whaling voyage to Antarctica, and it is claimed he was the first man to land on the Antarctic continent.

Louis Charles Bernacchi arrived in Australia from Belgium when he was young boy. As a member of the Southern Cross Antarctic expedition of 1898-1900, he became the first Australian to work and winter in Antarctica.

The Welsh geologist Tannatt William Edgeworth David took up the post of a geological surveyor in Sydney in his late twenties. He joined Shackleton's 1907-1909 *Nimrod* expedition and he was the leader of the first party to climb Mount Erebus. He was also with Mawson when he reached the South Magnetic Pole.

Two Australian geologists, T. Griffith Taylor and Frank Debenham, were with Scott on his *Terra Nova* expedition of 1910-12.

Mawson's Australasian Antarctic Expedition of 1911-1914 included a number of Australian scientists, and they would all spend two years in the Antarctic.

The photographer Frank Hurley was on Mawson's Australian Antarctic Expedition and one of the men put down on Elephant Island on Shackleton's Trans-Antarctic expedition in 1914-17.

In Shackleton's Ross Sea support party of the Trans-Antarctic expedition in 1914-17 there were several Australians; Keith Jack, Irvine Gaze, Lionel Hooke and a young man named Richard Richards.

It is arguable that all these Australians, from Borchgrevink to Richards, are heroes to some degree; that is, if we evaluate a person a hero if they have done something 'very brave or achieved something great'. (Cambridge Dictionary.)

However, if we classify a hero as a person who has exhibited an 'extreme heroic effort of great intensity, of a kind that is likely only to be undertaken to save a life', (Merriam-Webster Dictionary), there is only one of these Australians who displayed such heroic efforts as to save the lives of others; Richard Richards.

In 1914, Richard Richards abandoned his comfortable life as a science teacher in Australia, to travel to a very unfamiliar place; the Antarctic. He had no idea he would become embroiled in one of the greatest stories of endurance in the history of polar exploration and become a life-saving hero.

The Boy from Long Gully provides the reader with a thrilling insight into the mind-blowing and harrowing ordeal of twenty-two-year-old Richards. It is an utterly riveting story, one of the most amazing tales from a bygone era; the so-called Heroic Age in the Antarctic.

The book's content has been taken from diaries and books written by the people involved. Predominantly, conversations have been taken from diary transcripts and audio recordings by people in the story.

CHAPTER 1
Shackleton's aspirations

Sketch of Richards as a boy climbing a tree in the bush at Long Gully.

Two ten-year-old boys amble their way through the Australian bush. It is a hot day, a scorcher of a day, with temperatures above a hundred accompanied by hot northerly winds. Not that the heat or the wild winds really worry Richie Richards and his friend Jimmie. One-hundred-degree days with oppressive winds is not uncommon for early February, in central Victoria. A willy-willy swirls through the scrub, bending the tops of gums trees and rustling the undergrowth, but the boys simply shield their eyes from the dust and debris. The willy-willy quickly fades away.

The boys kick the ground as they dawdle along. There is no rush to get home from school. They pick up stones and stabkick them at an imaginary leading full forward of their favourite football team. They bowl stones, with Richards day-dreamily bowling googlies at an Englishman to win a Test match for Australia. They see ant's nests, with inch long bull-ants, and stir up the nest with a long stick, simply for their own amusement.

Then Richards spots a bird's nest, high up a towering eucalypt. He thinks it may be a kookaburra nest, although he knows they usually lay eggs in a tree trunk hollow. He tells his friend Jimmie he will climb the tree and see if there are any eggs, so Jimmie bunks him up to the first branch, and then watches as Richards shimmies up the trunk, from one branch to the next.

Before long, young Richie is high up the gum tree where he can clearly see the large bird's nest on the branch above him. Then the wind gusts wildly and the tree top bends markedly. His skinny schoolboy limbs hug the trunk tightly.

"Come on Richie, you can do it," yells his friend.

The boy bellows again: "One more branch and you will be there."

Richie pulls himself up another few feet, swings a leg out and hauls himself onto the branch. He pauses to suck a full breath in and to push a heavy breath out.

The nest is only five or six yards away so with both hands on the branch Richie gingerly slides his backside forward an inch or two, and then he carefully moves his hands on a little. He glances down at his friend on the ground, who looks very distant, then he slides forward a little more.

The wind bustles violently again, so Richie drops his chest to the branch and wraps his arms around it. With eyes tightly clenched his cheek kisses the bark and his arms bear-hug the branch. He waits for the wind to rest a little and then he continues, inching his way further along, praying the nest is not empty. His friend watches with trepidation.

There are three eggs in the nest, three large brown-spotted white eggs. They are kookaburra eggs and it is a rare find. Richie carefully pops one still-warm egg into his mouth and then inches his way back along the branch, backwards. When his back touches the tree trunk he carefully turns himself around on the branch, lowers one leg so it wraps around the trunk, and begins his descent.

He drops to the ground, opens his mouth and out plops the egg into his hand. The two boys stare at it because a kookaburra egg is a true prize. Blood trickles down Richie's legs, from tree truck scratches, but Jimmie says nothing. He would never have climbed that tree, not even for a kookaburra egg.

Richie finds a sharp twig, gently punctures both ends of the egg, and softly blows into one of the holes. Egg insides ooze out the other hole. The egg is added to other birds' eggs, all nestling on cotton wool in an old shoebox and the box goes back into Richie's school rucksack. He is quietly chuffed.

"How high up were you Richie?" asks Jimmie.

"Stand by the tree and let me work it out."

Richie walks about 20 yards away and then turns to face his friend. He holds up his thumb and then moves his thumb up the tree line, to the branch with the nest.

"You are four feet high Jimmie, and there are 22 of you to the branch, so that makes me 88 feet off the ground."

"You are good with sums Richie."

The two boys walk on through the bush, towards their homes in Long Gully, two miles away.

***

Why his parents named him so – with such a surname – Richard Richards was never quite sure, although his family called him Wally, his middle name. His friends at school called him Dick, or Rich, or Richie. He was born in 1893 on November 14 and as a boy he lived in Daly Street, Long Gully, a tiny rural community about three miles from the city of Bendigo in central Victoria.

Young Richards went to several schools in his early years, initially as a youngster of five years old at Long Gully, then to Raise Hill School about two miles away, followed by Violet State School, also in the area. After completing sixth class at the age of thirteen he attended a State Secondary school at Bendigo and two years on he sat for the Junior Public-School Exam. His high intellect shone through as he was awarded a scholarship to a teacher training institution at Carlton, in the corner of the Melbourne University campus. For the next three years, from the age of 16 to 18, he lived at the training college and studied science and mathematics at Melbourne University. After college, and now a young man, he was posted to various teaching positions in Victorian country regions, with his final appointment being at the Ballarat Junior Technical School.

***

A short dapper man looks flawlessly resplendent in his Navy officer uniform. It is Captain Aeneas Mackintosh, a handsome man even with a glass eye, although he is not tall, only a few inches over five feet.

It is the year of 1914, and Mackintosh is at home with his family, just prior to setting off from England for Sydney, and from there he will go to the Antarctic. His pregnant wife Gladys sits demurely on the living room sofa with her mother and a baby girl sleeps in a pram. His father-in-law speaks, gruffly.

"I hope you know what you are doing Aeneas. You have a steady job at the Service Guild in Liverpool."

"I know Sir," replies Mackintosh, "but I do not enjoy being stuck in a dirty office. I know I have not completed my work in the Antarctic, and I feel I must have one final wallow, for good or bad."

"He's a mad Irishman that Shackleton," says Aeneas's father-in-law. "He almost killed himself and three companions on his *Nimrod* Expedition of 07."

"I know Sir. But Shackleton was astute enough to turn back when he was only 100 miles from the South Pole. Coming back to base they were at the end of their supplies, except for some scraps of meat scraped off the bones of one of their horses that died on the trek south. But remember Sir, I was one of the men who put down food depots for him, which saved his life. He wants me to do the same job again."

Aeneas's father in law is not convinced.

"And now the bloody Norwegian Amundsen has beaten us to the South Pole, Shackleton still thinks it is worth going back there. What does he call it? The one remaining great object of Antarctic journeyings—the crossing of the South Polar continent from sea to sea. Tosh. That's what I say."

"But he has it all planed this time," says Aeneas. "I like its imposing name, the Imperial Trans-Antarctic Expedition. He is going to use two ships, the *Endurance* and the *Aurora*. The *Endurance* will take his party from Argentina to one side of the continent in the Weddell Sea. He will then set off aiming to reach the South Pole, come down the Beardmore Glacier and then continue to McMurdo Sound at the Ross Sea. Shackleton has appointed me to be the leader of his Ross Sea support party. I will have the second ship, the *Aurora*. We will sail from Hobart in Australia to the Ross Sea, establish camp at McMurdo Sound and lay a series of supply depots out to a hill called Mount Hope, at the foot of the Beardmore Glacier. Shackleton will need these depots to complete his crossing. He will be dependent on them."

His father-in-law shakes his head, but Mackintosh continues.

"Sir, there is no need to worry. We will be based at Scott's old hut at Cape Evans and all we must do is place food depots out to the Beardmore. The distance is only 350 or 360 miles. Sir Ernest says that he does not expect us to have any difficulties and I agree with him."

His father-in-law frowns: "Aeneas, I am concerned. You have a wife now, who is my only daughter, and you have a daughter of your own, and another child is on the way."

"Sir, I have an excellent crew. In Sydney we will take on a couple more Australian scientists to complete the team."

The father-in-law continues with his words of warning: "I do not want you to repeat that foolhardy behaviour of yours of five years ago. You had considerable luck then, when you and a sailor were caught on floating sea-ice and you almost lost your life."

"I am a lucky man Sir. I always have been."

His father in law is not impressed. He raises his voice.

"Make sure your luck does not run out as you have already used up two of your cat's lives. It was not only your escape from the ice, but you were lucky to only lose an eye when that cargo hook hit you in the face."

Mackintosh takes the baby from the pram and holds her up.

"I'll see you in two years my sweet girl."

Aeneas Mackintosh with his daughter before departing England in 1914, photo courtesy of Anne Phillips, granddaughter of Mackintosh.

***

Aeneas Mackintosh was born in India in 1879 but his early childhood was spent in Bedfordshire in England, where he attended Bedford Modern School. In 1895 at the age of 15 he left school to go to sea, serving as an apprentice on various merchant sailing ships before entering the P&O Service as a 5th Officer on the *Ballaarat* in 1900.

In 1907 he was recruited by Shackleton as second officer on the *Nimrod* Expedition to the Antarctic but unfortunately suffered a severe accident on arrival at McMurdo Sound. While assisting in unloading stores from the ship onto the shore, a crate hook attached to a barrel swung across and struck him in the right eye. The expedition's doctor found what appeared to be portion of a retina protruding through one eye. A sailor named Ernest Joyce who witnessed the incident told the doctor that he saw Mackintosh's lens lying on his cheek. The doctor successfully cut out his eye, but Mackintosh did not remain with the shore party in the Antarctic. He returned to New Zealand on the *Nimrod*. However, a year later he was back with a new glass eye and on his first exploit, where he attempted to cross from the ship to the shore on sea-ice, he almost lost his life. Other expedition members saw his actions at this time as 'nothing more than madness'.

On his return to England in 1909 at the conclusion of the *Nimrod* expedition Mackintosh's name was precluded from being appointed to any of the P&O Company's ships again, because of his loss of his eye. In 1912 he married Gladys Campbell at Holy Trinity Church in Bedford, his best man being the same doctor who operated on his eye in the Antarctic. Their first daughter Pamela was born in 1912 and in 1914 Gladys was expecting their second child.

In September of 1914 Mackintosh resigned from his position as assistant secretary to the Imperial Merchant Service Guild in Liverpool to join Shackleton's Imperial Trans-Antarctic Expedition. After appointing the 35-year-old Mackintosh as the leader of his support party Shackleton sent him several specific instructions, including:

...sail from Hobart about 1st Dec 1914 or in sufficient time to enable you to reach McMurdo Sound about the 1st of January 1915.

...at McMurdo Sound, as soon as possible, send out a party to the South. You will use your discretion as to who goes on this party. If you go yourself, you must have full reliance on your Chief Officer and make him for the time being Captain of the ship and second in Command.

....remember the main object of your expedition is for this party to establish depots out to Mount Hope at the foot of Beardmore Glacier in the south, in order to relieve, meet and assist my Trans-Continental party.

...my Trans-Continental party will rely on obtaining from your side enough provisions to carry us from Mount Hope to Hut Point.

Life for the boy from Long Gully is about to become intrinsically involved with Aeneas Mackintosh and also the sailor Ernest Joyce. In addition, Richards' life will be closely entwined with three other Englishmen: a padre the Reverend A.P. Spencer-Smith, a Navy Petty Officer Ernest Wild and a clerk Victor Hayward.

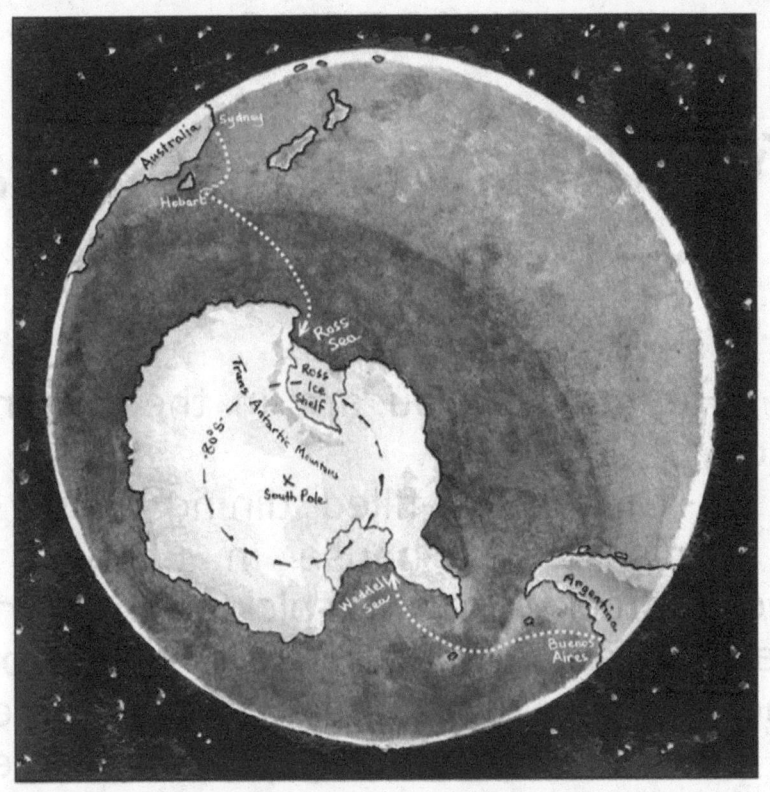

Shackleton's plans for his crossing of the Antarctic utilising a support party based at the Ross Sea.

CHAPTER 2

Two Petty Officers, a clerk and a padre

"Hey Joyce! You are in the papers. Today's Herald."

In the smoke-filled dining room of a men's lodging-house in Sydney, a short, stocky man is picking up dirty plates. He looks about forty years old and is even more unkempt than men at the tables; with a mop of unwashed tangled hair and an equally unkempt beard. It is Ernest Joyce, an ex-Petty Officer with the British Navy.

One man at a table has a newspaper, and as he holds it up Joyce attempts to take the paper off him, but the man waves Joyce away.

"Listen to this. It says here that a Sydney man, Mister E Joyce, who has been already on three expeditions to the south, has now received an invitation from Sir Ernest Shackleton to go again."

Another man at the table asks: "Is that you Joyce? We thought it was all bull telling us about going to the South Pole."

"That's right. Third time down south for me. I told you I was with Scott on his first journey, his Discovery trip. I fell in love with the place. My second journey was with Shackleton, on his Nimrod expedition. I reckon I saved Shacks life, with the food depots I put down for him. Now he wants me to help him again, while he walks across the continent. He will need provisions to get through the last stage of his trek, and I am the man he trusts to do the same job."

The man with the newspaper ignores Joyce. He continues: "You could be right Joycey. It says here that Joyce is with the Ross Sea Party, and another party at the Weddell Sea will be the transcontinental party."

Joyce interrupts: "Yes. Shackleton will be crossing the continent from the Weddell Sea."

"That's right," says the newspaper man. "The Ross Sea party will consist of six men, who will lay a depot at the foot of the Beardmore Glacier for the transcontinental party."

"I'm the leader of that party," says Joyce.

"Not so Joyce, from what it says here," says the man with the newspaper. "You are in charge of stores, sledges, and dogs, but an officer will be in command."

"That is bloody rot. I'll be in charge. Mackintosh is the officer they're talking about. The man will never get off the ship. He's a bloody fool."

The man with the newspaper is not listening.

"We all thought you might be living off tined food Joyce, but no. It says here that fresh meat is preferable to tinned meat, and is easily obtainable, from seals and penguins. Without this variety of food scurvy is almost certain to appear."

Joyce is irritated.

"I know. Of course I bloody know. I know what to eat. How to survive. Shackleton would have died in 09 without me. And I'll get him through this time."

The man reading the newspaper article continues to ignore Joyce.

"Hey, listen to this. In early days it used to take two hours to cook a breakfast, whereas now a meal is cooked in 20 minutes. In the old days, again, it would take an hour or two to build a snow hut to camp in at night; now tents can be put up in five minutes."

Joyce yells: "That bloody fool has never been there. Let him put up a tent in five minutes in a raging blizzard."

One of the other men at the table butts in: "Sounds like a piece of cake to me Joyce."

***

Ernest Joyce's naval career was similar in some respects to Mackintosh, although Joyce became a non-commissioned officer in the Royal Navy whereas Mackintosh was a commissioned officer in the Merchant Navy.

Joyce was born at Feltham, Sussex in southern England in 1875 and from the age of twelve he was educated at the Royal Hospital School at Greenwich,

England. At fifteen years of age he received his first posting in the Royal Navy. In 1901, after serving on several ships, he was with HMS *Gibraltar* at Simon's Town, Cape Town in South Africa when Scott's *Discovery* called there on route to the Antarctic. At that time Scott discharged three men and volunteers were called for as replacements and Joyce was among the four chosen from 400 volunteers. By this time Joyce had served 16 years in the Royal Navy.

Extract from Ernest Joyce's Naval Record.

In the Antarctic with Scott in 1901 Joyce was selected for the first sledging party onto the ice from the *Discovery*, and from there he put in more than 100 days sledging. Importantly he gained valuable experience not only in sledging, but in dog-driving in Antarctic conditions and with laying of supply depots in support of southbound parties. Other officers knew of Joyce's empathy with dogs and brought him back a set of dog's fangs from one of the dogs that had died out on the Barrier. Joyce had been the dog's keeper.

At the end of the expedition Scott declared that Joyce was one of his best men; 'a fine character, reliable in an emergency and a good sledging companion'. However, others did not see Joyce in the same light. One officer, when asked by Shackleton to join a later expedition declined, refusing to be associated with an expedition involving people of the 'Joyce type'. This may have been a reflection on Joyce's drinking habits, his working-class upbringing or his sometimes-boorish behaviour. Or a combination of such attributes.

Joyce was promoted to Petty Officer 1st Class in 1904, in recognition of his service in the *Discovery* Expedition.

Shackleton was with Scott on the 1901 *Discovery* Expedition and he had seen Joyce's work in the Antarctic, so he appointed him to oversee dogs and sledges on his 1907–1909 *Nimrod* expedition. Once again Joyce was involved in laying depots, this time for Shackleton's party attempting to reach and return safely from the South Pole. He led a support team (which included Aeneas Mackintosh) to lay supplies near a rocky promontory about 70 miles south from their huts at McMurdo Sound. This rocky promontory – called Minna Bluff – was first sighted during Scott's *Discovery* Expedition and became a key landmark and depot location for supply depots for southern journeys towards the South Pole. In late February 1909 Shackleton's party was struggling back north towards this Minna Bluff Depot. Shackleton wrote later that he and his men were at the end of their supplies, but he had faith in Joyce to lay food for him at the Minna Bluff Depot because in his words, 'Joyce knows his work well'.

Joyce did not return to the Royal Navy after the *Nimrod* expedition but worked in Australia, managing a lodging-house in Kent Street, Sydney;

an establishment whose clients were mainly wharf labourers and seafaring men, 'of a rather mixed character'.

In 1914 Joyce was 39 years old, eighteen years older than Richards, and an Antarctic veteran. His many years in the Navy, as a seaman and non-commissioned officer, had moulded his character; complete obedience to officers, loyalty, reliability when given a specific task, an ability to turn his hand to many things, a willingness to help, but also coupled with a lack of initiative and an inability to lead outside the set pattern of the Navy.

In March of 1914 he received a cablegram from Shackleton inviting him to join his Trans-Antarctic expedition, to which Joyce accepted. Shackleton then sent Joyce a follow up letter in July which confirmed Joyce's position as the person in charge of stores, sledges, and dogs, but the Ross Sea party would be commanded by an officer, to whom Joyce would be responsible.

Ernest Joyce.

***

Punts drift lazily down the River Cam at Cambridge on a balmy August evening, where elegant young women and handsome young men seem to prevail. Their muted voices blend with the gentle gurgling punt ripples. Arnold Patrick Spencer-Smith, known as AP or Smithy or padre to his friends, lies in one punt with his lengthy lithe limbs stretched out. He smiles at his two straw-boater wearing male companions, one who is punting while the other sits at Spencer-Smith's stockinged feet, massaging them.

"Why the Antarctic AP, and in a support party for Shackleton?" the punting man asks. "In my opinion there is no way he can cross the continent, so these depots you talk about putting down for him will never be needed."

Spencer-Smith smiles, draws on his cigarette and blows smoke skyward. He says nothing.

The angelic-faced young man massaging Spencer-Smith's feet speaks: "And you have just been ordained. You are now a man of the cloth, who can save souls in England. What souls are there to save at the South Pole, except penguins?"

The three young men laugh.

Spencer-Smith finally talks: "I have always longed for some adventure, ever since I was a young boy. Remember that lecture at Woodbridge? We must have all been about fifteen years old. It was on the voyage of Henry Hudson who perished in an attempt to reach the North Pole, and there was also the death of Sir John Franklin..."

The punting man interrupts: "From what I've read of the South Pole, and that is only Scott's journals, it is not a very nice place to die."

"Believe me that if anything does happen to me, I'll face it as cheerfully as I can. But I am really sure of seeing you both again – Deo volente."

The man massaging looks fondly at him.

"God will be willing padre. You are a good man."

The punting man shakes his head: "Death. Death. Death. That's all we ever read about from those places. Come back safely AP."

***

Spencer-Smith was born in London on March 17, 1883, joining a sister

Frederica and two brothers, and another brother and two sisters were born after him. His schooling was at a boy's boarding school, Woodbridge Grammar School in Suffolk, where he studied classics for six years.

In the winter of 1899, the young schoolboy Spencer-Smith paid the three-penny entrance fee to attend a lecture put on by the local Literary and Scientific Society, titled 'Arctic Travel & Adventure'. The lecture, by W.W. Mumford, touched on the travels of explorers in the Arctic regions, some who perished in their attempts to reach the North Pole and others who lost their lives searching for the North-West passage. Spencer-Smith wrote a report of the lecture for the 'Woodbridgian', his school magazine, mentioning explorers such as John & Sebastian Cabot, Henry Hudson and the sad tale of the death of Sir John Franklin. In his report Spencer-Smith outlined 'many difficulties & dangers' Mumford had elaborated on, and how they had to be overcome in such voyages of exploration. Spencer-Smith fascination with explorers travelling into polar lands was with him as a young boy.

Spencer-Smith passed University entrance examinations and then he attended King's College, London and Queen's College, Cambridge. He was a tall man; around six feet four inches in height, of slim build; 'slight but bony' claimed one magazine article of Queens College. Another article painted a picture of him as regularly smoking an 'inevitable' Woodbine, and that his 'lithe and lengthy form with a studious stoop' was a familiar sight in the courts of the College. However, he was known to have 'charming manners'.

Spencer-Smith went into teaching after University, at Merchiston Castle Preparatory School in Edinburgh, a boy's boarding school. In 1914, aged thirty-one, he was ordained as an Anglican priest, shortly before being selected to join Shackleton's Imperial Trans-Antarctic Expedition, as the chaplain and photographer in Mackintosh's support party. Shackleton wanted a priest as from experience he felt that there was a need for spiritual guidance and help to men in the lonely

Antarctic. Spencer-Smith was also chosen by Shackleton because of his sincerity, loyalty and his gift for getting along with people.

In mid-1914 Spencer-Smith left England for Australia on the steamer the *Ionic* with others of the support party and he was particularly looking forward to meeting one of his cousins Irvine Gaze, who lived in Sydney.

The motto of the Woodbridge School encouraged young boys to always focus their thoughts on aspects of life that are 'true', 'honourable', 'just' and 'pure'. During his time in the Antarctic, Spencer-Smith adhered to his old school motto, even in the most harrowing and trying of circumstances.

A.P. Spencer-Smith.

***

Two brothers, Frank and Ernest 'Tubby' Wild, are well-settled in a dimly lit corner of the Green Man, the lone public house in Eversholt, Bedfordshire. Their half-full brown beers wait to be consumed and both men add to the smoky atmosphere as they draw away on their pipes. There is little conversation, but after a prolonged pause Ernest speaks.

"I know you love it Frank. You must. How many times have you been there?"

"Three. And this will be my fourth."

"And you want me to join you? In this barmy thing where you and Shackleton are going to walk from one side to the other."

"I don't how to describe the place Ern. It's breathtaking. The Barrier. The ice shelf. The glaciers. The mountains. And there's no colour, nothing but black and white."

Ernest Wild listens as his brother goes on: "Then there's the silence, until a blizzard hits you. And the haunting feel of the place, that you are at the bottom of the world."

Franks suddenly starts laughing.

"Well, it is not so jolly all the time. I remember when we were talking to some military people in South Africa when we were on the way south with Shackleton and they asked: 'are you the fellows going to the South Pole? I'd give 1000 quid to be going with you."

Ernest smiles and shakes his head, but Frank keeps talking.

"Then, when we were sledging and the going was tough, I said to the chaps with me: 'what do you think you would sell your chance to that chap in South Africa now for?' and we all agreed it would be for less than a 1000 anyway. It was all self-inflicted so we couldn't really grouse."

But the 35-year-old Ernest Wild is unsure.

"Why would they want an old man like me anyway?"

Frank re-loads his pipe and lights it, as Ernest drains his beer.

"I will be walking across with Shackleton. You will be with the men putting down food depots for our last few hundred miles. Imagine meeting up at the Beardmore Glacier."

"Walking?" exclaims Ernest. "I am a sailor and I always have been, for twenty years."

"Dogs will do all the work Ern. They will be pulling the sledges. You know I've talked about Joyce; well he'll be in charge and he knows dogs. You will have trouble keeping up or more likely you will be probably just sitting on a sledge and getting a free ride most of the way."

Ernest smiles as Frank continues.

"It won't be hard for you Ern."

"Maybe. Easier said than done."

***

Frank Wild and Harry 'Ernest' Wild were two sons of the eleven children born to a schoolteacher and his seamstress wife in the late 1800s. The family lived in the village of Eversholt in Bedfordshire, a tiny parish consisting of little more than several clusters of houses, called 'Ends', and a church of St John the Baptist. The father was also the choirmaster at times and Ernest was in the church choir, reputedly with a good tenor voice and known as a person who could sing a comic song heartily.

By 1914, Ernest's brother Frank was well-known as an Antarctic explorer, having served (along with Joyce) on Scott's 1901 *Discovery* Expedition, with Joyce again and Mackintosh on Shackleton's 1907 *Nimrod* Expedition, and also in Douglas Mawson's 1911 Australian expedition to the Antarctic. In 1914 Shackleton had appointed Frank to be his second in command on his Imperial Trans-Antarctic expedition and it was expected that he would be with Shackleton crossing the continent. Hence, Frank Wild, like Shackleton, would be very reliant on the Ross Sea support party being able to put down food depots from Mount Hope to the huts at McMurdo Sound.

Ernest Wild.

Ernest had joined the Navy at 15 years of age and he then spent an uninterrupted 20 years on ships, advancing from Able Seaman to Petty

Officer 1st Class. As a Petty Officer he displayed a number of out-of-the-ordinary characteristics; he was popular with lower ranks because he did not use his rank to deal with minor infractions of regulations, he seemed to perform better in adversity rather than when things were travelling smoothly, and Naval officers found they could trust him to complete a given task, without fuss, and without seeking any notoriety.

Ernest Wild was only three inches over five feet tall. He was always known as 'Tubby', which had come about because he was short and looked heavy. In 1914, at 35 years old, he was serving on the *Pembroke* when the Navy approved for him to be lent for service with Shackleton's Imperial Trans-Antarctic Expedition.

Extract from Ernest Wild's Naval Record.

***

As an indication of his boyhood imagination, ten-year-old Victor Hayward chooses as a Sunday School prize the book *World of Ice* by RM Ballantyne. It is easy to imagine a young boy in London England in the late 1800s being entranced by Ballantyne's tale of men in the Arctic, such as when he describes two teams of men, with their dogs and sledges setting out:

> One party was to take the largest sledge, and the whole team of dogs, on which, with twelve days' provisions and their sleeping-bags,

they were to proceed northward ... It was a clear, cold, and beautiful starlight day, and the snow gave forth that sharp, dry, crunching sound, under the heels of the men as they moved about, that denotes intense frost.

***

A couple embrace. The tall, broad frame of Victor Hayward holds his fiancé Ethel tightly as she snuggles closer, and then she raises her head for Victor to gently touch her lips with his own.

"I'll be back in a year my dear."

Ethel clings on, even more tightly.

"And I'll keep a diary, and every day I'll write to you and tell you how much I am missing you."

Her soft reply carries doubt: "But the dangers."

"There are no dangers so do not worry. As soon as I return, we shall get married and then we will be together for the remainder of our lives. I promise you."

"I do not know why you have to go and why you are giving up the good position you have here in London."

"It will be a hard life I know, but I will be quite content. I have the satisfaction of knowing that I will be actually engaged in something important. Sir Ernest's life will depend on the depots we will put down."

Ethel sighs as Victor continues.

"I know you can't understand what all this means to me, going down there, away from you..."

His voice breaks.

"When do you actually leave?" asks Ethel.

"In two weeks. Sir Ernest is coming down to the docks to see us off. The ship will arrive in Sydney, Australia in December and then we plan to be at McMurdo Sound in the Ross Sea by early January. We will then be sledging and laying depots for a couple of months, living at a hut during winter, as there will be no light and too cold to be outside. We will resume sledging in October and expect to meet Sir Ernest coming across in February of the following year. We will then return to Sydney in March, and from there, a dead homer for me, you bet."

In September of 1914 Hayward and his parents meet Shackleton before Victor departs, and Shackleton remarks to Mrs. Hayward: "I'm not going to give your son much hard work to do."

To which Hayward replies: "But surely, Sir Ernest, this isn't going to fizzle out into a picnic – I could get that at home."

***

Victor ('Vic') Hayward was born at Harlesden, London in 1887 into a very large family; he had eight sisters and five brothers. At the age of twenty he travelled to Canada with his brother Leopold, aboard the 'Empress of Britain', looking for adventure in a cold climate. He arrived at Calgary in March of 1907 and worked on a ranch in northern Canada, gaining experience as a sledge driver with working dogs before he returned to England in November of that year.

In August of 1914 he became engaged to a Miss Ethel Bridson, whose family also lived in the inner north-west suburbs of London.

On his return from Canada he had found settling back into an office routine very difficult, and like many young men in Britain at the time, he was entranced by the exploits of Scott and Shackleton in the Antarctic. When the opportunity came in 1914 to apply for a position with Shackleton's newly announced expedition, he offered to 'do anything' to secure a place. His time in the northern wastes of Canada and particularly his dog-driving experiences secured him a position.

Victor Hayward.

On August 28, 1914 he received a letter signed by Shackleton, confirming his appointment, and that he was to report for duty on September 14. His local paper the Willesden Chronicle reported news of his appointment:

Sir Ernest Shackleton has appointed as a member of the Imperial Trans-Antarctic Expedition. Mr. Victor George Hayward, the fifth son of Mr. Frank Checkly Hayward, one of the oldest residents of Harlesden. Mr. V.G. Hayward and a number of other members of the expedition will sail on the White Star Line steamer the Ionic from Tilbury on the 13th inst for Hobart Tasmania. Where they will embark on the Aurora for McMurdo Sound. We feel sure that Mr. Hayward's many local friends will wish him good luck and a safe return.

Victor Hayward was about to realize a long-held dream, to undertake a dangerous adventure into a world of ice.

***

Life on the R.M.S. *Ionic* travelling from England to Australia is idyllic for Hayward, Wild and Spencer-Smith. Other men of Mackintosh's support party are on board too, and include Stenhouse, who is Mackintosh's second in command and Chief Officer of the ship that will travel to the Antarctic, the *Aurora*. They will pick up the *Aurora* in Sydney.

The men on the *Ionic* turn out at 5am, and some like Hayward and Wild attend to the dogs that are destined for the Antarctic. There are 26 dogs on board. Breakfast is at 8.30, classes in activities such as Signalling and Seamanship follow on most days, there is lunch at 1.30, more classes in the afternoon, the feeding of the dogs at five then dinner at seven.

They are travelling saloon class with wonderfully comfortable quarters and fill up their spare time in the usual passenger way; playing deck games, tug-of-war competitions, sports days, and lounging in the sun reading.

In October 1914 the dogs – now only 18 in number as eight have died before reaching Australia – are dropped off at the Quarantine Station in Hobart. They will be picked up later, after two months quarantine. The ship sails on to Sydney where the men are put up at the Australia Hotel, and Spencer-Smith meets Mackintosh for the first time.

"What is he like padre?" asks Hayward when he catches up with Spencer-Smith.

"An absolute dear. Such a neat, wee chap, with a gold eyeglass in his remaining eye, and an Oxford voice."

Spencer-Smith goes on: "He is a glutton for work and very cheery. I think we will all, staff and men, fall absolutely in love with him."

Hayward has an interview with Mackintosh and is appointed Secretary to the expedition. He then works with Joyce on the myriad of administrative tasks still to be completed; purchasing items such as '10 crates of Dog Biscuits containing 1 cwt as a donation' from one firm, who were very interested in 'Mr. Joyces verdict' when they returned. The biscuits contained a large percentage of yeast extract and the makers thought they would 'give a good account of themselves in the Artic' [sic].

At the Australia Hotel in Sydney they have a meal table to themselves, with Captain Mackintosh at the head and Spencer-Smith at the foot. Spencer-Smith is absolutely delighted when Mackintosh calls out at the start of dinner: "Padre, say grace, please!"

He thinks his chaplain's work will be appreciated and supported by Mackintosh.

Newspapers announce the arrival of the support party in Sydney. It is exciting news for the Australian public:

SHACKLETON EXPEDITION.
ROSS SEA SECTION,
ROOM FOR AUSTRALIANS,
SYDNEY, Tuesday. -Most of the members of the Ross Sea section of Sir Ernest Shackleton's expedition have reached Sydney. This section, which is under the command of Captain A.F. Mackintosh, of the Royal Naval Reserve, is to go south in the Aurora, and make bases for Sir Ernest Shackleton's party which will start from the Weddell Sea and cross the Antarctic continent to the Ross Sea. The party hopes to get away from Sydney by the end of the present month. The Aurora will return to Hobart before finally setting out on her journey south.

A pampered life continues for Mackintosh and his men whilst at the

Australia Hotel in Sydney. On Monday November 16, 1914 the hotel produces an embossed Dinner Menu card for the men, and it is titled:

MENU

The Imperial Trans-Antarctic Expedition.

'Toasts' to the King, the Royal Family, the Expedition and to Sir Ernest Shackleton, the Captain and to Visitors.

'Codfish, oyster sauce, sirloin with cabbage and boiled potatoes, Pheasant, cheddar & Stilton, Plum duff & brandy sauce'.

Spencer-Smith signs his copy of the menu, and has others – Mackintosh, Hayward and Stevens and more – sign it too and then he posts it off to his parents, with a long letter extolling the pleasure of being in Sydney. He writes:

"We took the Aurora out of dock yesterday to allow work below the waterline to be finished. She looks splendid in the water and we are all tremendously proud of her and

longing to feel the beat of the engines."

"We broke off at 12 yesterday and I went with The Captain and Stenhouse for lunch with officers of the P.O. Medina, the ship that took King George around the world, the most luxurious appointed 'hotel' you can imagine. We had a jolly time."

He tells his parents: *By the way, Stenhouse and I have a favourite song: "Wish me mother could see me now."*

CHAPTER 3
The boy from Long Gully signs on

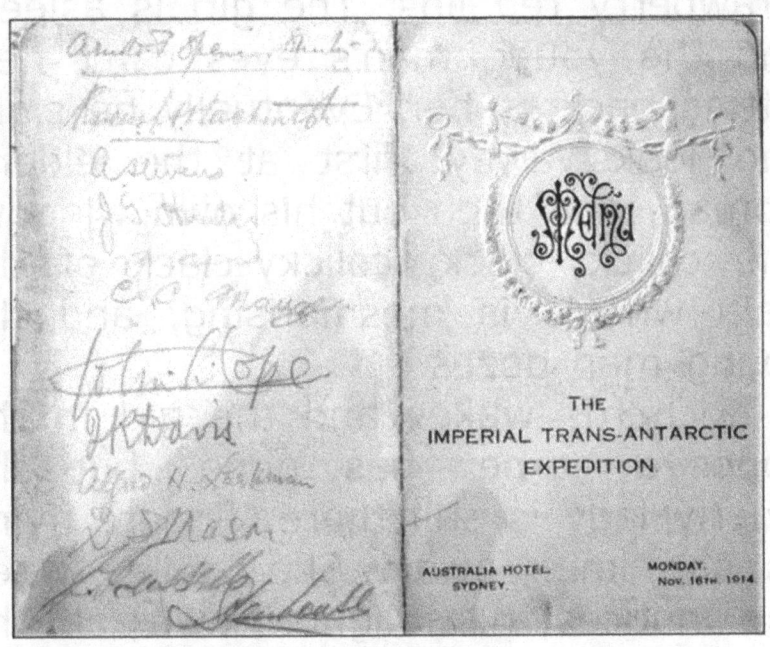

The dinner menu at the Australia Hotel in Sydney, November 14, 1914.

Scraggly gum trees of the grey brown Australian bush flash by. Warm December sun streams in the railway carriage window.

An elderly lady knits, and she smiles warmly when the personable young man opposite looks her way, but his attention is focussed on a young lady in the opposite corner of the carriage. The young man is Richard Richards and he is hypnotised by the most beautiful girl he has ever seen; jet-black ringlets of hair, faintly freckled cheeks and strawberry red lips. The girl is asleep, and the young man's eyes can't help flitting back to her. Eventually he sighs and looks away, first at the elderly woman, and then out his own window. The colicky-clack, colicky-clack of the train wheels is mesmerising, and the young man dozes.

Richards wakes and the girl in the opposite corner has gone, but the elderly lady is still there, fingers flying as she knits away. She smiles when she notices his slight frown at the empty seat.

"The girl left us at Wangaratta."

He says nothing.

"Where are you from young man?"

"Long Gully ma'am. It is a small country town near Bendigo."

"And, where are you going?"

"To Sydney, ma'am."

"And, why are you going to Sydney, may I ask?"

"I have an interview for a position, with a Captain Mackintosh. He is taking a ship to the Antarctic and wants two or three Australian scientists to join him. He is the leader of a support party at the Ross Sea for Shackleton, the Irish explorer, you may have heard of him. He is going to walk across the Antarctic continent."

The lady smiles. "I think we all know of Shackleton, and Scott of course, and our own Douglas Mawson. You are a scientist?"

"A physicist ma'am."

"Good luck with the interview young man. And good luck if you go to the Antarctic."

Richards in 1914.

***

On Saturday November 21, 1914, an advertisement in a country newspaper, the Mount Alexander Mail, had caught Richards' eye:

A surgeon is required for the Imperial Trans-Antarctic Expedition, at a salary of £150 a year; also a physicist, at a nominal salary of £1 per week. Both would be expected to assist with scientific work outside of their special sphere and to undertake any duties arising out of the activities of the expedition. Applications are invited from graduates and applications should be addressed as soon as possible to the commander, Aeneas Mackintosh, S.Y., Aurora.

Richards' understanding of Shackleton's Imperial Trans-Antarctic expedition was that it was to be the last big journey to be made in Antarctica; to cross the continent, a journey comparable to going across Australia in distance. He was intrigued.

Around that time, other Australian newspapers had announced the arrival of the *Aurora* in Sydney, that there were positions open to join the expedition, the *Aurora* was at present undergoing an overhaul at Cockatoo Dock, and the party hoped to get away from Sydney by the end of November.

On seeing the advertisement for a physicist Richards acted immediately and wrote to Mackintosh.

Junior Technical School
104 Doveton Street
Ballarat

Nov 21 1914
The Commander
S.Y. Aurora

Sir,
I have the honor to apply for the position of Physicist to Antarctic Expedition.
I have completed two years' work in each of the following subjects at the Melbourne University—Natural Philosophy, Pure Mathematics & Applied Mathematics.
My age is 22. At present I am engaged in the instructional staff at the above school.
I have the honor to be,
Your obedient servant
R.W. Richards.

Within a couple of days, he received a telegram signed "Mackintosh" asking

him to come to Sydney for an interview, with his expenses paid. However, Richards baulked at the opportunity. He sent back a telegram, advising Mackintosh that it was not easy for him to make the trip:
26/11/1914

Sir,

I have found it extremely difficult to obtain relief from duty at this time of the year and at short notice, examinations press and the staff is undermanned.

My qualifications I have already provided. These can be substantiated by the Melbourne University. In regard to health I beg to state that to the best of my belief it is excellent. I have always been athletically inclined.

In regard to testimonials I could arrange better if I know what particular specialization in science work is required.

Richards heard nothing for four days, so he started to fret, that he may be overlooked for the position. He then sent another telegram:

30 Nov 1914

> *Difficult to find relief from duty until twelve December.*
> *Arrive Sydney fourteenth December.*
> *Wire immediately if suit.*
> *Anxious not to lose chance.*
> *Send instructions.*

He followed this telegram with another, detailing his qualifications and health:

2 Dec 1914

> *Natural philosophy, one and two.*
> *Pure and mixed mathematics, one and two.*
> *Melbourne University certificate university.*
> *Health excellent, athletic state.*
> *Public servant.*
> *Height five feet nine inches.*
> *Weight eleven stone ten pounds.*

He finally received a reply to these telegrams, again telling him to come to

Sydney, expenses paid. His interview was to be on the *Aurora,* which he knew about, as it was Australia's most famous Antarctic explorer Douglas Mawson's old ship, and the Navy was overhauling it.

***

Richards is shocked. After being lulled on a ferry trip across Sydney Harbour, with the bay at its most alluring, he steps onto the naval dockyard at Cockatoo Island. In front of him is the *Aurora,* the ship that is going to the Antarctic. His first reaction is that he would not be anxious to go much further than Sydney Heads in what seems like a most inadequate craft.

However, Richards' fears were unfounded as the S.Y. *Aurora* had already proven to be a suitable vessel for conditions in polar regions. She was a steam yacht, built in Dundee in 1876, 165 feet long with a 30-foot beam, by the same shipbuilders that constructed the *Terra Nova* and *Nimrod.* Because the ship was registered with the Royal Yacht Squadron loading restriction regulations would not apply when she left a port. This would be essential because when she eventually left Australia her decks were covered with cargo, and livestock. With crews of over 60 men she was used as a whaler in the Arctic, from 1876 to 1911 and then she was purchased for the first Australasian Antarctic expedition of Douglas Mawson. The ships masts were converted so a smaller crew could be employed and to also improve its performance in winds while carrying considerable cargo. In early 1914, Shackleton bought the *Aurora* for his support party of his Imperial Trans-Antarctic expedition.

Richards climbs the steep narrow gangway of the *Aurora* and a salt of the sea sailor watches the smartly dressed young man come aboard.

"Excuse me, sir," calls Richards. "I'm looking for a Captain Mackintosh."

"Through that door laddie, down the steps, and straight ahead is the wardroom. Mind your head."

Richards bends low as he goes down the companionway, walks along the passage and enters an ill-lit darkly timbered wardroom. Three men are seated behind a small desk and one of them calls to him, in a crisp, clipped English accent: "What do you want?"

"My name is Richard Richards and I have an appointment to see Captain Mackintosh."

The man with the clipped accent is a small man, dressed in Navy Officers uniform, and Richards cannot help but notice his glass eye.

Aeneas Mackintosh.

"Richards. Yes. Sit down. I am Mackintosh and this is padre Spencer-Smith," as he waves at the man on his left, and then nodding at the other man: "this is Stevens, my chief scientist. You say you are a Physicist."

"Yes sir. I majored in Natural Philosophy, with Pure Mathematics and Applied Mathematics, at Melbourne University. I'm currently teaching at a Technical School."

Mackintosh does not seem concerned with Richards' scholastic abilities.

"Are you fit? Healthy? Can you do hard work?"

Richards is surprised by the questions, but unconcerned. He tells Mackintosh he is healthy; however, he avoids mentioning a rupture that had been sustained at football the previous season. Under medical advice Richards still uses a trust.

"I'm fit sir, very strong in the legs. I play football, cricket, and walk everywhere, rather than ride a horse."

"Excellent. As well as doing scientific work, you will be required to help my men at times, and the work can be back breaking. You may be running with the dogs when they do the sledge pulling, but you will also be pushing and pulling a sledge yourself, loading and unloading provisions and putting up tents in the fiercest of winds. The temperature will be well below freezing. Are you up to it?"

"Yes sir. I do not want to miss the chance."

Mackintosh turns to the men each side of him and asks if they have any questions. Spencer-Smith speaks softly: "Why do you want to go to the Antarctic? It will not be a holiday."

"I'm a sort of restless chap," Richards replies, "and I'm pretty fed up with teaching."

Mackintosh interrupts.

"Today is December the fifteenth and we leave from Hobart in two weeks. Can you get yourself to Hobart before Christmas?"

Richards stares at Mackintosh. He is little stunned, because he seems to have been accepted for the job, after such a short interview, but he quickly replies.

"Yes sir."

Mackintosh pushes forward a single sheet of paper, titled Imperial Trans-Antarctic Expedition Agreement.

"Here is Shackleton's standard Agreement, which you have to sign. You will be paid a salary of fifty-two pounds a year. It is a normal agreement for such an enterprise but note that you must obey all commands and not publish anything without Shackleton's written consent."

Richards quickly looks over the words of the Agreement and signs it.

"Buy some Jaeger and Burberry," says Spencer-Smith as Richards stands up to leave. Richards frowns and it is clear he does not understand, so Spencer-Smith elaborates.

"Jaeger is woollen clothing made by a London firm and likewise Burberry is a London firm that makes outer garments. They use a woven fabric that breathes to stop sweat building up, which freezes."

"It will be very cold Richards," Mackintosh warns him.

Richards is now a member of Mackintosh's Ross Sea support party, which will travel to the Antarctic on the *Aurora*. He returns home to Long Gully to prepare for his adventure, simply telling his parents: "I am going to Antarctica."

In the short time Richards has to collect his gear he manages to buy some warm clothes, including a cold weather jacket from *'Morsheads, Gents and Ladies Tailors, Ballarat'*. The only reading material he packs is the magazine NATURE, A Weekly Illustrated Journal of Science, of November 1910 to March 1911. This magazine contains a series of articles on the physics of the swing and swerve of a cricket ball, a topic of interest to the sports-minded young man. He says his farewells to his family, and travels to Hobart by ship from Melbourne.

While in Sydney, Mackintosh recruits three other Australians who are to be with Richards for some of his time in the Antarctic; Irvine Gaze (Spencer-Smith's cousin) who is taken on as a commissariat officer and general assistant, a scientist Keith Jack, and Lionel Hooke as the wireless operator.

Unlike Mackintosh and Joyce who know the Antarctic and conditions they will be living and working under, Richards has no more than a vague idea of what life will be like. However, he is young and healthy and not concerned that life may be a little difficult, even dangerous. He is quietly confident that his main role will be to conduct scientific experiments for one or two years, and help Mackintosh with his depot laying activities, as and when needed, but he expects this may only be occasionally.

The *Aurora* leaves Sydney for Hobart on December 15, 1914 and on board are Mackintosh, Joyce, Hayward, Spencer-Smith and others of the Ross Sea support party. All of the men are eagerly looking forward to the time when a start may be made to the Antarctic.

***

Richards is impressed: "Bloody big dogs."

"Huskies," Hayward tells him. "Like the dogs I have worked with before, in Canada."

Richards, Hayward and Joyce lean on the *Aurora's* railing and watch as two men bring a large number of dogs on board.

Joyce points at one of the two men: "See the tubby one? That is Ernie Wild, but everyone calls him Tubby. He's a brother of Shackleton's right-hand man Frank and I hope he's as good as Frank."

The *Aurora* is at the Hobart Quarantine Station taking on board Ernest Wild, Aubrey Ninnis, and eighteen dogs. Richards had arrived in Hobart a week before and found the *Aurora* moored to a wharf where confusion reigned, with cargo all over the place and men rushing everywhere. He helped load stores, with other Australians recently added to Mackintosh's party, Jack, Gaze and Hooke.

To Richards' land-lived eyes the ship appeared horribly overladen, with a heavy deck cargo of coal and cases of petrol stacked on the top of the cook's galley, and on deck. It was quite impossible to get any meals on board so when there was a brief let up with work, he and the other men simply ran across to rather dubious establishments on the waterfront, to satisfy their hunger. During loading there was no room to stay on board, so Richards stayed with others in what he felt were very sleazy quarters near the docks.

Joyce turns to Richards. "If you are ever feeling lonely down south, go out and say hello to one of the dogs. They'll always be pleased to see you."

Joyce loves talking about the dogs: "They weigh about 70 and 80 pounds each and they're the most efficient mode of traction. Each of them can draw a load of over 100 pounds, and they eat only a pound of food a day. Dog biscuits."

"Where do they sleep, in the snow?" asks Richards.

"Yes. They've no shelter. We just tie them up by chains to a long steel cable, giving them a little movement of a few yards but never too close to each other. I remember in the *Discovery* Expedition of fifteen years ago, when we first took our dogs onto the ice. Captain Scott thought it would be a good plan to give the dogs a run, so we landed them, but we forgot the wolf nature of the hounds. They formed a ring with the victims in the centre, and there were several killed before we got to them."

"They're not dangerous to us, just the opposite," points out Hayward. "Always very eager for work."

"That's right Vic. They'll rush up to you and even try and insert their head into the loop of a harness if you are carrying one. You will see, after a night's sleeping, they'll watch the tent, and when we start preparing to start, they'll be yelping all the time. They're so keen to be off."

"How do they know where to go?" enquires Richards.

Joyce shakes his head. "They don't. They need something to follow, unless they've been out and are heading back to somewhere they've been. Usually a man will walk ahead and then they will have something to see and follow. But they're not so smart. If there's a mirage up ahead, say a snow cairn, they cock their ears and their footsteps quicken. I think they see the mirage as a penguin or a seal."

Richards takes it all in, as Joyce goes on.

"When they're out in a blizzard they simply lie down and coil around, the drift covers them and after a time they're completely buried, in compact snow."

"How do they get out?"

"They can't and they've no chance whatever of freeing themselves. They need us to dig them out."

Richards, the scientist, cannot fathom that out.

"Sounds like that is against the laws of nature."

***

On the evening of December 24, 1914, the Governor of Tasmania comes to see the *Aurora* leave and a tremendous crowd at the docks wave the ship and the men on board goodbye. The departure was reported in the Hobart newspaper 'The Mercury'.

The Ross Sea members of Sir Ernest Shackleton's Antarctic expedition made their final departure from Hobart in the auxiliary barquentine Aurora at 6.30am on Thursday (December 24th).

Richards and the others all wave to the people as the *Aurora* moves away from the wharf.

"Wave goodbye to the girls Richy," says Hayward, "It is going to be some time before we see them again.

"You know, I have never spoken to a man from any Antarctic expedition that was not in love with Australia and New Zealand," says Joyce. "Where else will you find such hospitable people? The people are enthusiastic about expeditions. You are a hero without having done anything."

22-year-old Richards, the Australian, is now with the five Englishmen who are to become an integral part of his life in the Antarctic. There is the ship's captain and expedition leader 36-year-old Aeneas Mackintosh, 40-year-old Antarctic veteran Ernest Joyce, fellow Petty Officer Ernest Wild who was the same age as Mackintosh, 30-year-old Reverend A.P. Spencer-Smith and Victor Hayward at 28 years of age.

Others on board who will play a less significant role in Richards' life for the next two years are Stenhouse the first officer of the *Aurora,* Stevens the chief scientist, Cope a biologist and the medical officer, Ninnis who had come aboard with Wild with the dogs, and the other Australians, Jack, Gaze and Hooke. The ship's crew included three other officers and nine lesser ranks; Able seamen, stokers, the cook and a steward.

There are two weeks of sea travel ahead before the *Aurora* will reach the Antarctic, a voyage of 2500 miles; from Hobart at latitude of 42° 88' S to McMurdo Sound in the Ross Sea at latitude of 77° 84' S.

The First World War had broken out in that year, in August of 1914, and this was in December, and here was an expedition going down to the Antarctic in the middle of what was to become a terrible war. However, in those years, in those months, no one thought much about the war. Richards for example certainly didn't. He like most of the others had the idea the war would be over soon because the papers then were full of news of the Russian Steamroller steamrolling across Europe and the Germans would not have any chance. No one on board the *Aurora* really thought the war would last beyond Christmas and some of the crew and staff were terribly worried the war would be over before they even got back to England.

CHAPTER 4

The voice of Caruso in the Antarctic

The virgin ocean-traveller Richards finds the *Aurora* to be a very unstable ship. It rolls like a cork, up to 30 degrees to each side when there is a large swell or high wave. At times Richards is so nauseated he cannot go below; all he can do is lie on a hatch on deck. In rough seas he finds it to be worse at night-time as there are no lights. His sleeping quarters on board are a far cry from anything he has ever experienced; far worse than the sleazy place he stayed in at Hobart. His own bunk, and those of five others, is right over the upsweep of the ship's counter, and is only reachable by using cleats nailed to the steep upward slope of the deck there. The sleeping place is a narrow slot-like region, only about two feet high, and three men sleep side by side. The man whose bunk is farthest astern must get in first; otherwise it is quite a feat to try to crawl over the outer two sleepers with the narrow head room available. Washing is done with seawater, using basic primitive facilities, by simply hauling up a cask of water from the sea. The lavatories discharge into the sea a few feet above the water line, and, when the ship is rolling heavily, sea water gushes up through the opening to the occasional discomfort of the individual caught.

At a meal break in the mess room Richards sits with Joyce, Wild and Hayward, but the two Navy men see nothing unusual in the rough seas. Not so Richards, as he holds tightly onto his meal plate and mug to stop them slipping off the table.

"This ship is very near turning over."

Joyce smiles: "Just a good roll Richie, nothing more."

"Just a good roll? Just before I came up, I was sent flying into my bunk. And do you see what trouble the steward has bringing us food from the kitchen."

"Galley, Rich, not a kitchen," says Wild, also with a smile.

"All right, galley. He has a hell of a time running from the galley where the food is cooked down the length of the ship and then up a few steps to us down the back."

Joyce and Wild laugh at Richards' innocence with naval terms. Wild tries to explain: "Aft Rich. The steward is laying aft, not down the back."

"Where are you from Rich?", asks Joyce. "The big smoke, or the bush, with the kangaroos?"

"A bush town Joycey. Called Long Gully. Very small town it is too. I used to walk to and from school every day, like all the kids at Long Gully. Very few families with bicycles when I was a boy, except the penny farthing type. All of us people who lived in small rural communities had to make our own way everywhere."

Wild is interested in the young Australian. "Big family Rich?" he asks. "Not like mine, I hope. There were eleven of us."

"Just two brothers and two sisters for me," says Richards. "And we lived a very close community life. Pretty religious too as my father was a verger of the local church. The All Saints Anglican Cathedral."

"So, we are the first people from your mother country you have met?" asks Hayward.

"Not quite Vic. Bendigo mining was at its heyday when I was a boy. There were mines everywhere with huge muck heaps of slag around them, Anyway, most of the miners had come out from Britain and particularly Cornwall but there were also Chinese miners. At times I used to watch the Chinamen working over the surface 'tailings' or dumped soil from old claims that you British miners had discarded."

Wild, the man who has lived on ships for the past twenty years is curious. "And what did you in the bush?"

"Like all of us in isolated towns, we had to make up our own amusement. Although there was fire brigade practice on the weekend and football games in the winter."

Hayward interrupts. "Fire brigade practice? What is that?"

"It was always done on Sunday mornings. We would take a water wagon to the football oval and pretend there was a fire. Often, we had competitions with the brigade from a town nearby. Someone would ring a bell and the teams had to unroll the hose, connect the water, start the generator, and a lead man would climb up a ladder onto something like a shed roof, and the first one to spray water was the winner. All done to make us faster fire fighters."

Hayward smiles. "And football Rich? You play football in Australia?"

"We call it Australian Rules football, not your round ball game. Then there were cricket games on Saturday afternoon in the summer. Ten years ago, when I was a boy, Long Gully did not have even a picture theatre. No artificial methods of amusement. Me and my friends simply made our own."

There is no conversation for a short time, then Hayward brings Richards' thoughts back to the present.

"Sleep deprivation is my problem here Richie," he says. "I find it to be an incredibly noisy place. The wailing wind never stops, and the dogs keep howling with their throaty howl." Hayward is not enjoying the voyage.

Wild offers him some words of condolence: "You get used to it Vic. In a wooden ship you hear every roar of the water on the side. Seems like there is nothing between you and the sea."

Hayward nods: "Last night the boat rolled absolutely rotten. I turned in at ten, but she rolled so much I did not sleep five minutes."

"I find I am perpetually wet," says Richards. "The leaky deck rains down on me when I am below. And when I am on deck, I am sure to be caught out by a sea at any time I move from one place to another."

Wild laughs: "And there is no question of changing your wet clothes for dry Richy. It can't be done."

Richards listens closely to Joyce's additional words of advice: "Better in your bunk than on deck Richy as it can be dangerous outside. The wind will get so strong further south it can lift a man off his feet."

No matter how unwell Richards feels, he must work when ordered. There is work in the engine room, taking a turn at watch, and there are tasks to carry out on deck, such as pulling in the halyard when they must trim the sails. If there is a strong wind and the sails need to be adjusted all available hands are called on deck to man a rope, and the boson chants a sea shanty, so all the men work in unison. The young man from the bush town of Long Gully is entranced by the sailors singing sea shanties. He soon learns it is a most effective way to utilize the ship's manpower. As the sailors sing, they know on which beat to start pulling: "O Shenandoah! I LONG to hear you", "O Shenandoah, I LOVE your daughter", and they all pull there. Richards realizes they could pull on a 1-2-3 call, but he is sure that it would be nowhere near as effective pulling the ropes in time to a shanty.

The *Aurora's* only stop to Antarctica is at Macquarie Island where they land stores and livestock for the staff. A meteorological station had been established there during Douglas Mawson's expedition a year or two earlier

At Macquarie Island Hayward sends a radio telegram to his fiancé Ethel Bridson at Crownhill Road, Harlesden,

England, telling her that 'Everything OK. Just leaving Macquarie.' He also writes a letter to his father, telling how much he is enjoying the adventure so far:

> *On the S.Y. Aurora, at sea, bound for the Antarctic, via macauqirie [sic] Island. We have had glorious weather since leaving Hobart.*

He spells out to his father what he expects will happen when they arrive at the Antarctic, concluding with the phrase 'dead homer', signifying he will head straight home when the work is complete.

> *Arrive McMurdo Sound middle of January, sledging, laying depots til end of April, living at hut from May till September, resume sledging operations in October; expect Shackleton through in February 1916; return to Hobart or Sydney in March 1916 and then a dead homer, you bet.*

Mackintosh sends a letter to his wife, telling her of the glorious weather they have had so far, and that the ship is simply slipping through the water. He explains that he could even be in a farmyard instead of a ship, with dogs barking, sheep bleating and cocks crowing. Richards does not write a letter or send a telegram.

Joyce and Wild go ashore at Macquarie and kill several seals, primarily for dog food, but Joyce uses the opportunity to pass on some of his Antarctic knowledge to the young man Richards.

"Richie. There'll be seal meat on the menu tonight and you must try and eat it. You must get to like it."

Richards nods. He is happy to go along with the words of wisdom from Joyce, the Antarctic authority in Richards' eyes.

"The seal flesh is excellent, but its liver, kidney and heart are delicacies. Down south it will be the only fresh meat available, except for a few penguins now and again, and fresh meat is the only way to stop scurvy. It must be cooked bloody rare, so we don't lose any of its goodness."

"I have tried seal meat," says Hayward, "and find it unappetising."

"Ignore him Richie. Seal is like beef. And penguin breasts are just like wild duck."

***

Richards listens to Mackintosh and Spencer-Smith. It is a few days after leaving Macquarie Island and the three men are on the bridge, where Richards feels less sea-sick outside in the fresh air, as cold as it is.

Spencer-Smith queries Mackintosh: "How are we travelling Skipper? You said Shackleton wanted us to be there by the start of January."

"We are making excellent progress padre. The ship is doing about one mile an hour, but we will be a month late, close to the end of January I am sorry to say. Which means we only have two months at best to lay some depots before winter sets in, just in case Sir Ernest does come across this year. Although I doubt it."

"We seem to be bowling along."

"The old girl is behaving admirably. She rides along the waves in fine style although she is lurching about a good deal this evening. Much to my disgust as my cabin has been wet twice by seas breaking over the poop and finding their way into the cabin through the door."

Mackintosh notices Richards staring at birds following the ship.

"Whale birds Richards. I saw my first albatross yesterday, and this afternoon a flight of Antarctic petrels."

The young man Richards, in a strange new world for the first time, has a question for Mackintosh: "When do we start to see ice?"

"Anytime. From now on we keep a strict vigilance." He then looks around at the sky.

"Beautiful clouds. How I'd love to show Gladys all these sights! And how she'd love them too! Indeed, then I would consider everything complete."

"It would be nice to get some news from home," says Spencer-Smith.

"Right. Just to know how the loved ones are faring. That's the only drawback to this job. I had hoped to send wireless messages off today, but Hooke is having problems."

Later in the day, Richards is in the mess-room working with Hayward,

Joyce, Wild and others and they are making boots, because insufficient supplies had been shipped from London to Hobart.

"What do you call these boots we are making Joycey?" asks Richards.

"Our own patent Antarctic boot made up from canvas and sennit rope soles. We do not have enough finneskoe boots."

Hayward is happy to impart some of his knowledge: "Do you know of finneskoe boots Richie? They are normally made from reindeer-skin, with the fur on the outside and Sennegrass – a Norwegian dried hay with insulation and moisture absorbing properties – on the inside."

Joyce is not happy: "But some bugger mucked up our order in London and we only have finneskoe for 10 men, instead of 16."

Hayward mentions that they did buy extra boots in Sydney, but Joyce is not impressed.

"Wretched sea boots they are too Vic. My feet are constantly wet. It's a pity the maker is not here wearing them himself."

The men laugh at the thought.

***

"Pull Rich. Pull," screeches Victor Hayward.

"I am bloody pulling. What do you think I'm doing?"

On the voyage south, Richards, like all the non-crew men, is allocated tasks, and he finds one job to be very difficult. At times, he and Hayward are told to go on deck and haul up the coal ashes from the boiler room down below and dump them in the sea. On every watch, the ashes from the boilers are raked out on a plate and sprinkled with a hose to cool them down. Then they are shovelled into huge cylindrical buckets, three or four high and about 18 inches in diameter. A rope goes up a ventilator to the deck and where two men get on a pulley and heave up the bucket with the ashes, which are damp, and very heavy.

The ship dips and another huge wave engulfs the two young men.

"Like getting a smack with a whitewashed wall," yells Hayward.

Richards and Hayward are clad in oilskins from head to foot, but they are white all over, because they are being sprayed continually by waves and the water freezes immediately on their clothes. They brace themselves as they hold onto the pulley rope. Both men are breathing heavily. Richards suggests if they wait until the ship is leaning down as it dips into the swell, it will be easier to pull, because the rope won't be vertical. The *Aurora* dives into a swell and spray engulfs the ship. Richards and Hayward are covered completely by the wave as it comes over. Richards yells: "Pull. Pull. Pull," and the pulley rope moves a couple of feet.

The ship comes up to the top of the swell, steadies herself and then she dives down again. The two men yell to each other: "Pull. Pull. Pull."

Finally, a bucket at the end of the pulley rope appears and it is full of damp coal ash. Richards and Hayward grab hold of its handle, haul it out of the shaft and onto the deck. Puffing furiously, they drag the bucket over to the ship's edge, lean it against the railing, and then lift it up and tip the contents overboard.

"Only about a dozen of these before we are done apparently," explains Hayward. "Pretty simple job really, but its hard work. Better than being down in the boiler room."

After hauling up another bucket of ashes, Richards shakes his head, but he is philosophical.

"Not what I thought I would be doing. So much for scientific work, like taking meteorological readings."

"Me neither Rich. I should be looking after the dogs."

"That's right. You worked with them in Canada, didn't you?"

"I was only twenty when I went there, seven years ago. I was with one of my many brothers, and we worked on a ranch in northern Canada, working with dogs. I learnt to be a good dog driver."

"Many brothers?" Richards queries.

"I am in a large family, five brothers and eight sisters. Would believe that my parents only married after the birth of the last?"

"What were you doing before now?"

"Working as a produce clerk, in London, and living at home. When I received a letter confirming my appointment from Shackleton, my parents showed it to the local paper, the Willesden Chronicle it is called, and they ran an article."

"So, you are famous?" Richards jokes.

"Hardly. They wrote more about my mother and father, that I was the fifth son of Mister Frank Checkley Hayward, one of the oldest residents of Harlesden. They wrote that my many local friends wished me good luck and a safe return. Ethel was very pleased to read it though."

"Ethel?" enquires Richards. 'Who's Ethel?"

"My fiancée. We became engaged last August. I won't be able to send her any letters now we are past Macquarie, but Mackintosh said they will be giving us dairies when we arrive at the Cape Evans hut, so I will make a diary note for her, on just how heavy a bucket of ashes is."

Richards' mind flicks back to the girl with strawberry red lips on the train, and he muses for a few seconds over what might have happened if he had asked for her address, so he could write to her.

He queries Hayward.

"Dairies? I can't imagine there being anything so exciting happening down south that it would warrant keeping a diary."

After an hour of hauling up buckets of ashes, Richards is exhausted, so dead-tired that he drops down on the nearest piece of covered deck and is asleep in an instant. Then, he is woken in what seems like the next instance, to be called for a two-hour watch. There, one of the sailors gives him a drink in a pannikin, taken from a keg. Richards looks at the liquid and frowns: "This looks like dirty water to me."

However, he takes a sip, and then asks for more, feeling better all the time. The sailor laughs.

"Water? Was no water laddie. The best navy rum."

The sailor turns to his companions and calls out: "Hey chaps, here's an Australian who mistakes rum for water.

Next time we may as well give him sulphuric acid."

***

A dozen men are crammed into the wardroom of the *Aurora*. Mackintosh has called a meeting, to outline his plans for when the ship arrives at McMurdo Sound in the Ross Sea.

The taller men, Richards, Hayward and Spencer-Smith stand behind Joyce and Wild and others. Richards understands from what Mackintosh is saying that there are two huts at McMurdo Sound, one at Cape Evans, and another hut 13-mile further south at Hut Point. Mackintosh tells the men that these huts are near latitude 78 degrees south, and their task is to lay major depots at each degree of latitude south from there; that is at 79 degrees south, 80, 81, 82 and 83 south, and then a final depot by a small mountain named Mount Hope, at the foot of the Beardmore Glacier. Each depot will be about 70 miles apart. Mackintosh is confident that if the work is done correctly, Shackleton would then have food and fuel to use on his final 360 miles. Mackintosh stresses to the men that Shackleton is 100 per cent dependent on these depots.

He then outlines his timetable. He expects the *Aurora* to arrive at McMurdo Sound at the end of January, and depot laying will commence straight away. Teams of three men plus the dogs will be employed, but early sledging will only last for two months, February and March, before winter sets in. The second and main season of sledging will be after winter, from October through to February in the following year, in the Antarctic summer.

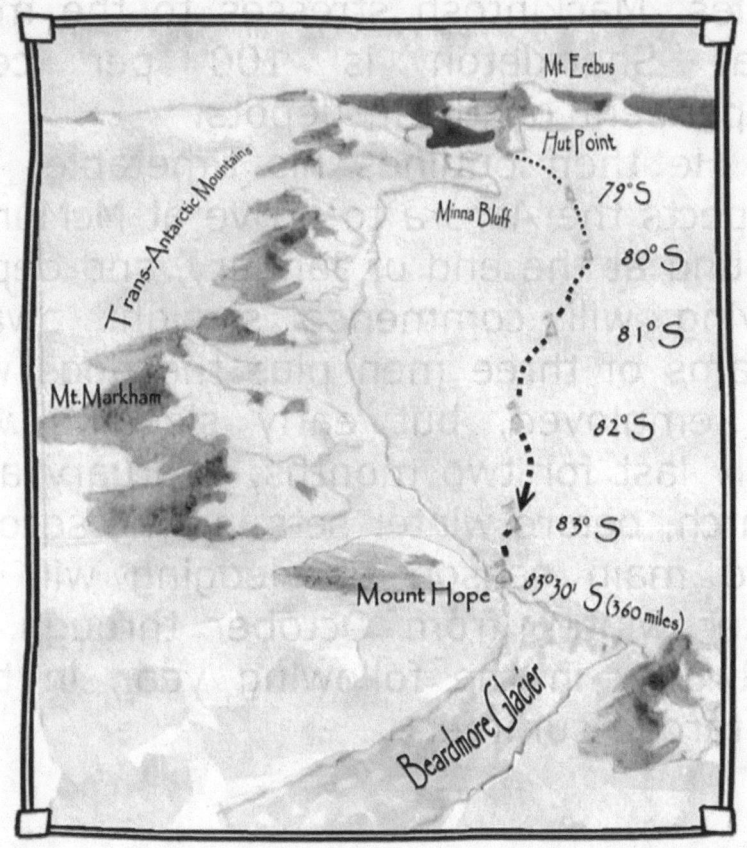

Planned depot locations out to Mount Hope.

Richards overhears Joyce muttering to Wild: "He's a bloody idiot. Why does he want to take the dogs out as soon as we arrive?"

Mackintosh looks at Joyce.

"Questions Joyce?"

"Sir, I feel we'll be jeopardizing the dogs by taking them out straight away. That wasn't Shackleton's original plan. They're getting no exercise on the ship, owing to the small amount of space, and they're unhealthy from the continual soakings from the sea water."

"We have to use them Joyce."

Joyce shakes his head and mutters to Wild in his almost verbose and slightly bombastic way of talking: "If I had Shacks here, I would make him see my way of arguing but Mack is my boss and I must uphold him. As he won't take my advice about the dogs, I must let him have his way."

Mackintosh goes on, telling the men that the ship will not return to Australia, he will winter her at Cape Evans. Joyce speaks quietly to Wild again, and Richards listens attentively.

"He's more than a bloody idiot. He is a damn fool. Why does he want to leave the ship there over winter? This is the silliest damn rot I've ever heard. We should unload everything into the huts and send the ship back to Australia or New Zealand for the winter."

"Sir, I'm not in favour of wintering the ship," says Joyce out loud. "Scott did winter the *Discovery* but then we had no experience of Antarctic conditions."

"It will be fine Joyce. The ship will be well sheltered at Cape Evans."

He tells the men that it is Scott's old hut at Cape Evans, and this hut would be the base for the scientists, but most of the men and the crew would stay on board the *Aurora*. Joyce is not happy. Once again Richards hears him talking quietly to Wild.

"Anyway, Mack shouldn't even be sledging, he should stay on the ship. He'll soon find that he's not fit to carry out the hard and tedious work that is in front of us. Having one eye will play merry hell with him in the extreme temperatures."

Richards is not sure whether Joyce is right or if Macintosh is right. That is, should they start using the dogs straight away, and should the ship stay at McMurdo Sound for the winter? Both of Mackintosh's decisions will have a major impact on Richards' life in the Antarctic.

***

Richards is in a new world, an almost silent world. After days of being battered by shrieking winds in huge seas – through latitudes 40°S, 50°S and 60°S in the Southern Ocean – the *Aurora* has passed latitude 70° and now there is only a soft wind and a gentle swell of the sea. The ship starts to pass icebergs and ice floes moving up from the south and the dull droning of the ship's engine prevails.

Richards finds the relative silence particularly striking and weird. He stands with Spencer-Smith and Wild at the bow of the ship where slushy snow and ice cover the decks and rigging, and icicles hang from every projection. The three men watch as the ice floes gradually thicken into pack ice.

The *Aurora* guardedly edges her way through, shuddering when she hits a floe, where there is a loud crack, but the ship moves on. It does not become trapped, unlike Shackleton's *Endurance* in the Weddell Sea on the opposite side of the continent.

The ship clears the pack ice and is then into the calm waters of the Ross Sea. The Ross Sea is by the Antarctic continent and is known as the silent sea, because of the solitude of the vast expanse of open water that is met after coming down through the wild seas of the Southern Ocean.

Joyce joins these three men for a while and he points out the varying wildlife; the Antarctic petrel and snowy petrel, Weddell seals, crab-eater seals asleep at the edge of a floe or rolling and wallowing in and out of the water. There are Adelie penguins and emperor penguins, some basking in the sunlight on ice floes near the ship. They see whales, hundreds of them and Richards estimates some are 25 to 30 feet long. He is overwhelmed when they rise close to the ship.

The *Aurora* steams slowly south into the even calmer waters of McMurdo Sound in the southern sector of the Ross Sea. McMurdo Sound is a famous inlet, the gateway to the South, where Scott first visited in 1901. Its most southerly shore is the Ross Ice Shelf and its eastern shore is Ross Island, on which there are three volcanoes, Mount Terror, Mount Terra Nova and Mount Erebus. The first two are extinct, but Mount Erebus is an active volcano rising steeply some 13,000ft. from sea level and it is ice covered right up to the crater.

In 1901 Scott established his base on Ross Island, at a location he named as Hut Point where his men built a storage shed, *Discovery* hut. Hut Point was – and still is – the most southerly part a ship could go, because of the Ross Ice Shelf, which never goes out to sea. (The ice shelf was also known as the Barrier or the Great Ice Barrier, as it prevented sailing further south.) When Scott returned to McMurdo Sound in 1911, he built another hut on Ross Island, at Cape Evans, a sheltered inlet to the north of Hut Point.

The huts are located by the edge of the sea and only 13 miles apart but to travel between the two locations is difficult, because icebound rocky cliffs and impassable glaciers follow the coastline from Hut Point round to Cape Evans. Travel between the two locations by ship is only possible for a few weeks in February, when there is water at the base of McMurdo Sound. For the other eleven months of the year McMurdo Sound is largely frozen over with sea-ice. This means that for most of the year there is only one practical way to travel between Cape Evans and Hut Point, and that is on foot over the sea-ice. However, the journey on foot can only be made safely in the late winter months, when sea-ice is thick.

(At times over the next two years, these two huts, the *Discovery* hut at Hut Point and the hut at Cape Evans, will be sanctuaries for Richards and his companions.)

***

Mackintosh comes forward to stand with Richards, Spencer-Smith and Wild.

"Look at that scenery," he says, "and those clouds? Are they not simply beautiful? Like some gigantic drop scene, so delicately outlined. It would make an artist's mouth water to have them to paint."

Mount Erebus

The crusty twenty-year seaman Wild is no romantic, but even he is taken in by the view. He points: "That must be Erebus Skipper, about eight miles distance I reckon."

"There is a cloud hanging over its peak," replies Mackintosh," but you can see a stream of smoke coming up from the crater. That mountain will be a welcoming landmark as we return from laying the depots."

Richards stares at the wall of ice ahead to the south, the Great Ice Barrier. It is an impenetrable wall over 100 feet high in places, extending for hundreds of miles in both directions. Then his eyes are drawn further south where he can see the blue outline of peaks of the Trans-Antarctic Mountains in the far distance. They are an imposing range of mountains running roughly south – north across the Antarctic continent for about 1,000 miles, where some peaks rise to 15,000ft. He knows the Beardmore Glacier is in those mountains, where the furthest depot is to be laid for Shackleton.

The ship moves closer to Ross Island where the huts are located. There, peaceful white snow covers the island's slopes and the snow slopes gradually descend into the sea, where black rock protrusions of steep perpendicular cliffs at the sea edge provide a contrast of colour.

Richards is taken by the scene: "It would be quite impossible for me to give even a faint impression of the wonder and beauty of this place to people back home. Mack, I now know how people like you and Joyce are drawn back here."

"And that is despite the hardships and risks Richards. There's a fascination about the life here that I think would appeal to almost anybody."

The Aurora at the Great Ice Barrier.

"It's astonishing. I have already forgotten the outer world."

Mackintosh raises an issue that he is familiar with: "But there will come times when you simply long for civilization again with its attendant comfort and luxury. But these fits don't last, and you thank your lucky stars that you're down here, living a real life."

Suddenly, Joyce's voice booms from the crow's nest.

"Richie. Come up here. Thousands of penguins. You can see them over the cliffs of the Barrier."

Richards climbs the main mast to be with Joyce, eighty-five feet above the deck and the two of them gaze out at the immense shelf of ice, stretching for hundreds of miles to the south, the Great Ice Barrier.

"Are those seals?" asks Richards, pointing at a collection of black dots.

Joyce nods. "That's our food Richie. Seal meat. You will love it after a day's work down here."

Richards then points at the ice cliffs ahead.

"There is nowhere to land, with that wall of ice."

"We'll go to the huts and land there. The only way to reach the Barrier is to leg it from Hut Point."

Then, the ship's engines are cut. All the men on deck are hushed so Richards and Joyce stop talking as the

ship glides slowly and noiselessly forward. Suddenly, the silence is broken by the sound of a tenor voice:
> *Qui dove il mare luccica*
> *E tira forte il vento...*

It is Caruso. The seamen have set up a gramophone on the stern.

The young man from Long Gully is hypnotised by the perfection of the moment, with its absolute stillness; and by Caruso's voice. He has arrived in the Antarctic.

CHAPTER 5

Man-hauling a sledge and 'hoosh'

Scott's chair and table at the Cape Evans hut.

"This is eerie," says Richards.

His eyes are drawn to a table and chair in one corner and he sees a book on the table. It is Scott's table. Three Australians, Richards, Jack and Gaze with an Englishman Cope have just entered the hut at Cape Evans. They presume Scott was reading the book before he left on his fatal journey to the South Pole on his 1910-1913 *Terra Nova* Expedition. Nothing else in the hut appears to have changed since that time. Biscuits lie on the large dining table, tins of vegetables, labelled as McDoddie – the London manufacturer – line the shelves, wall hooks hold drinking mugs, ruffled sleeping bags lie on the bunks and images of Scott, Wilson, Bowers and Oates flash through Richards' mind.

On January 24, 1915, thick sea-ice had prevented the *Aurora* reaching Hut Point at the base of McMurdo Sound, so the ship was tied up to the ice edge between the two huts, about four miles to the south of Cape Evans, and nine miles to the north of Hut Point. The dogs are taken ashore for exercise and then Richards joins some of the others on the sea-ice where they try their skills at skiing across the ice to visit the Cape Evans hut.

Dogs being unloaded off the Aurora at McMurdo Sound.

The hut is located near the beach and Richards finds the various surroundings to be magnificent. Westward, across the 20 or so miles over McMurdo Sound, he sees a majestic range of mountains, the Trans-Antarctic Mountains Range. The view in that direction is spectacular, as the mountains stretch as far as he can see. Then, when he turns and looks to the North and East, he is overawed by the imposing height of the active volcano Mount Erebus, with its continuous plume of smoke. The summit of Erebus seems to be on top of him as he stands outside the hut.

Others, including Mackintosh and Wild, ski down to the hut at Hut Point, and when they return to the *Aurora* Richards talks to Wild.

"What is the *Discovery* hut like Tubby? We've just been to one at Cape Evans. I could feel the ghost of Scott there."

"No ghosts at the hut at Hut Point. It is just a shed. No heating. No bunks. Nothing but an old blubber stove, and not much else. We lit some seal blubber in it and the smoke drove everybody out except Stenhouse and Stevens. They're Scotch so they could stick it."

Richards laughs.

***

On the deck of the *Aurora*, Mackintosh stands with Joyce in front of Richards, Wild, Spencer-Smith, Hayward, Cope, Stevens, Jack, Gaze, Ninnis and Hooke.

"I want Joyce to talk to you about sledging. As you know, he has been here twice before, with Scott and with Shackleton. He is back in very familiar territory, having set up depots between Hut Point and the Minna Bluff location for Shackleton."

"Thank you, Sir," says Joyce. "With the exception of the Skipper here who accompanied me on a journey for Shackleton none of you have any experience with sledging down south. I'll give some good advice on different subjects such as sea-ice, avalanches, frostbite, snow blindness and others. Now the Skipper knows about the dangers of sea-ice from when he was here a few years ago."

"That's right Joyce. A sailor and I were hauling a sledge from the *Nimrod* to the shore and we camped for the night on the sea-ice as the shore was too far to make in one day. On the next day the ice we were on started moving rapidly. The whole ice sheet had formed into flows."

"What happened Skipper?" asks two of the men simultaneously.

"We were lucky. We made land."

None of the men talk. They let Mackintosh's flirtation with death by being taken out to sea on floating sea-ice sink in. Then Joyce continues.

"Now, I'll be laying the course to the Minna Bluff and I'll be marking the way by cairns and flags as one is liable to find crevasses. In those areas keep yourselves roped together. Some crevasses have overhanging snow-curtains and you can easily walk over the edge, especially when you are coming from the north in thick weather."

Joyce then tells the men of his firsthand experience with frostbite.

"I was with Scott on his *Discovery* voyage, and in September at the end of winter I was out with others on the Barrier laying supply depots. One night the mercury in the thermometer sank to below minus sixty-seven. I said to my two pals in the tent that I thought one of my feet had gone and when I took my boot off, I found my foot was white to the ankle. It took over an hour before my tent mates could get any sign of life going, and they only managed this by putting my bare frozen foot under their jackets on their chests."

Richards, as well as the other Australians, Gaze, Jack and Hooke, are becoming a little uneasy with these stories.

Joyce continues. "Now, your tents. Don't forget to pile enough snow on the skirting of your tent, every time you put it up. Wind can suddenly spring up, so you need the tent to be very secure. There's nothing worse than waking up in the middle of the night to find you are lying in a snow drift with your tent blown away. You won't even be able to see your tent mates."

"I have camped in the snow in Canada," says Hayward. "I found that even if you leave a single portion of the skirting showing above the snow the blizzard will find any such spot and use it as a lever to work its way under and into the tent. Then the insides fill up with a thick powdery snow which covers everything."

Hayward pauses, so Joyce goes on.

"A few more things to be aware of. Wear your goggles, otherwise you can get snow-blind and it is very painful. If you do get snow-blind while we are on the march all you can do is wrap a cloth around your face and walk blind. It can be cured by taking cocaine drops that night. Food. If you can, eat fresh seal meat, as much as you can to stop scurvy. We all know scurvy killed Scott and his men. The only cure is fresh food. And finally, be careful. When you get to Hut Point, you will see a hill which has a cross on it. It is Vince's Cross, in memory of George Vince who was a member of the *Discovery* Expedition. The first man to lose his life in this region. He simply slipped off the edge of the ice and rocks and fell into the sea."

Richards looks around at the others, and like he, they are starting to feel a little apprehensive as to what may lie ahead.

***

Dogs fret. They bark and howl, eager to be on the move.

Mackintosh, Spencer-Smith and Wild are harnessed up to a sledge, with a team of nine dogs. It is the first run to take stores from the ship to Hut Point over the sea-ice, about nine miles away to the south.

Richards asks Joyce: "Why only three men? Why can't others go too?"

"All to do with the tents and the food Rich. Tents are designed to hold three men, so food has been packed for teams of three men. The rationing is critical. Daily doses of pemmican and biscuits."

Richards interrupts.

"Remind me. Joycey, what is this pemmican?"

"A mixture of dried beef and fat. With hot water and biscuits, which are like sailor's hardtack biscuits, it becomes our hoosh. Hoosh is the staple food for all Antarctic explorers."

Joyce goes on.

"So, daily doses of pemmican and biscuits for three men have been sorted into a linen bag, and seven of these have been put in a canvas food tank. We see a canvas food tank and we know that it holds enough provisions for three men for one week. Under all circumstances, a canvas food tank has to last a week."

Richards still wants answers: "But why a week?"

"Because depots, like the ones we'll have to put down, are located about 70 miles apart, at each degree of latitude, and we should march 70 miles in a week."

"It's normal to walk 70 miles in a week?" asks Richards.

"Yes. Unless a blizzard hits."

Joyce then laughs. "Or you fall into a crevasse."

All the men and crew are there with Mackintosh, Spencer-Smith and Wild, helping with the last lashings on the sledge, adjusting dogs' harnesses to stop them fighting, or simply watching.

The lead dog is Nigger and as soon as his trace is attached on the sledge everything is ready to go. Nigger stands still, legs splayed out. The order is called to start but all the dogs make a wild dash at each other, furiously biting their partners. The sledge does not move.

Another try is made, after adjusting the tangle the dogs have put themselves into. Mackintosh, Spencer-Smith and Wild each lead a dog and progress is made, for a short while, but once again, a bundle of dogs start fighting with each other.

A third and a fourth try is made and then at last, with the three men sitting on the sledge, they move off respectfully. There is a parting shout and three cheers, and before long Mackintosh, Spencer-Smith and Wild and their dogs are moving away.

The sledge moves well at first, but then it stops, because one of the dogs has decided to turn back towards the ship. There is chaos. A riot. A mass of rolling, struggling fur and fury of dogs fighting. Mackintosh, Spencer-Smith and Wild beat the dogs to separate them, and eventually they move on once again.

Most of the men return to their duties, but Richards stays watching. He is very envious of the three men heading off on what seems to him to be an exciting and adventurous jaunt. Slowly, Mackintosh, Spencer-Smith and

Wild, their dogs and the sledge, all merge into one black dot on the white ice. Then it starts to snow, and everything becomes obscured, so Richards turns away.

This three-man team of Mackintosh, Spencer-Smith and Wild will remain intact for the majority of the depot laying, right through to March of the following year. Mackintosh appoints Spencer-Smith to the cook in their party, Wild to look after the dogs – while they use them at this stage – and he nominates himself as the navigator and handyman.

***

Sketch of Richards standing by a fully laden sledge.

Hands on hips, a doubting Richards scrutinises what he and two other men are expected to haul; a sledge laden with boxes of provisions that are to be taken out to a depot location on the Barrier. In addition to the provisions, there is a Primus stove, spare parts for the stove, cooking pots, three pannikins and spoons, an axe and a shovel, three sleeping bags, a tent, three sets of skis and sticks, plus spares such as bamboo sticks, lashings, bunting and safety pins. They also have stored away an extra pair of boots each: finneskoe boots. They have kerosene fuel for the stove, and methylated spirits which is used to prime the stove. Other personal clothing includes pairs of socks and additional mitts made of fur, which are hung around their shoulders by a lamp-wick.

For three men, including the sledge, their personal gear and equipment is a total weight of around 200 pounds, but they also have to take their own food allowance, and the provisions to be depoted. (Each canvas tank bag with seven days food for three men weighs nearly 45lb.)

Richards is about to set off on his first sledging run, where he is with five men, in two teams of three, each team pulling a sledge. These two teams have been instructed to put down food and fuel at nominated depot locations close to Hut Point.

"Hayward, Richards and Ninnis. Are you ready?" calls out Cope who is in charge. "Stevens and Hooke and I'll follow you with the second sledge. Harness up."

These two teams do not have dogs, they are to man-haul two fully laden sledges from Hut Point up onto the Great Ice Barrier. Richards tries to put on his harness, a broad waistband of double canvas, pierced at the back and fitted with an eye through which an alpine rope passes, leading back to the sledge.

"All the weight will be taken by the waistband Rich," says Hayward as he comes over to help. He has hauled sledges before, when he was in Canada. "It is only suspended from the shoulders by these straps," which he attaches to a buckle fixed to Richards belt.

"Go," calls Cope.

"One, two three, pull," says Hayward to Richards and Ninnis. They pull but the three of them cannot move their sledge. It is too heavy.

"One, two three, pull," calls Cope to his two companions, Stevens and Hooke, but they cannot move their sledge either.

Cope realises they will have to relay. "The six of us on one sledge, take it forward and all return for the second. Twice the distance but it's the only way."

Richards tells Hayward it is not twice but three times as far, because they must go out, back and then out again.

It is three miles for every one gained. The six men do manage to haul one sledge through the foot-deep snow, where they find the most heartbreaking part is getting started. Some of the team have to swing the sledge to get a smooth starting place and to break the frozen runners. Then they heave back the sledge with one hand, keeping up the swinging with the other, and then someone calls 'Go' and with a mighty heave from everyone the sledge starts moving. It often takes three repetitions of this before the men pulling have a strain on their traces. Off they move, utterly breathless, but they plug on through the unyielding snow, until their combined energies give out, so they rest, before starting again.

Richards hears Hayward mutter: "I now know what utter exhaustion is!"

As well as the physical aspect, Richards quickly learns of the awkwardness of man-hauling a sledge in the snow. For example, a toilet break comes when one man perceives an uncertain feeling in his stomach. That man calls a halt, with an apology, and then he quickly fumbles around to undo the leather strapping of his sledge harness. He then walks away from the others, although they all turn to keep their back to him, then the man doing his toilet loosens the lamp wick that secures his windproof outer garments and squats. Naturally, in the extreme cold of sub-zero temperatures, he tries to expose as little flesh as possible.

To add to their difficulties there is a wind into their faces at times and the tears from their eyes run down their faces and freeze onto their snow goggles. Richards wears his goggles religiously and fortunately he is not affected by snow-blindness.

What Richards does notice though is that after it has snowed for some time, and snow drifts have built up, small objects such as a tiny piece of string or a piece of biscuit remain uncovered with snow. He thinks this is extraordinary and cannot work out why it happens, as there is sometimes a foot of snow everywhere.

***

Richards stares at the blue flames.

"I read about the cheery hum of the Primus. It's quite mesmerising."

Richards, Hayward and the third man in their team Ninnis are sharing a tent. It is an older style tent and to erect it six bamboo poles have to be slotted into a heavy canvas pole cap. When the poles are up the canvas skin of the tent is quickly hauled over the frame by two men. The other man races around placing blocks of ice or snow on the skirting of the tent, before the wind lifts the canvas up and off the frame. They erect the tent at lunch breaks too, to provide protection from the weather.

Richards is the nominated cook one evening and he tells Hayward and Ninnis that he has a new recipe: "Smithy gave me a special recipe for what he called his Hoosh deluxe. Listen to this: it is a mug of pemmican, mixed with six lumps of sugar, some salt, nine spoonful of oatmeal and six crushed biscuits."

Sketch of three men using their Nansen cooker.

Cooking is done on a Nansen cooker, designed by the Norwegian Arctic explorer Fridtjof Nansen, and along with the tent and their sleeping bags, it is a most critical competent of their gear. Richards is intrigued by the efficiency and simplicity of the cooker. There are a number of parts; a shallow dish for the primus stove, then two pots, one inside the other, with one lid covering both pots. The meal is cooked in the inner one, and snow melted in the outer one and this allows for food to be cooked and snow melted simultaneously. Plus, an outer cover is lowered (gently) over the whole apparatus to keep in as much heat as possible. A small amount of methylated spirit is poured into a cup at the base of the stove, lit and when it is almost burnt up an air-valve is screwed up and a few tentative pumps made at the kerosene. With patience, and practice, they manage to have the right mixture of kerosene vapour and air rushing up, and finally the burner rings are surrounded by a halo of intensely hot bluish flame.

Before Richards starts to serve out the hoosh, Hayward tells him of a sledging game called Shut Eye.

"It's a method of dividing up the food that ensures a fair distribution Rich. You, as the cook, pour out roughly equal portions into each of our three bowls."

After Richards has poured out the three portions, Hayward tells him to turn around and Hayward then points to one of the bowls.

"Whose?"

Richards understands, and call out: "Yours."

Hayward points to another bowl.

"Whose?" he says again.

"Shackleton made up the game Richie," says Hayward as they start eating. "He saw men staring at each other's portions, as if one had deliberately received a bigger portion."

Richards, Hayward and Ninnis do not undress for sleeping, but turn in fully clothed after removing their boots. Even though temperatures remain below freezing, inside their sleeping bags they are not cold as it is still 'summer', in early February.

In the mornings Richards finds he is very good at waking himself at the correct hour. He shakes himself out of his bag, calls out to Hayward and Ninnis, goes outside to fill up the cooker with snow and passes it in to Ninnis, who is usually up before Hayward. Ninnis gets the primus going and within 30 minutes they have their morning 'hoosh', which creates a fine warming tingle down their bodies.

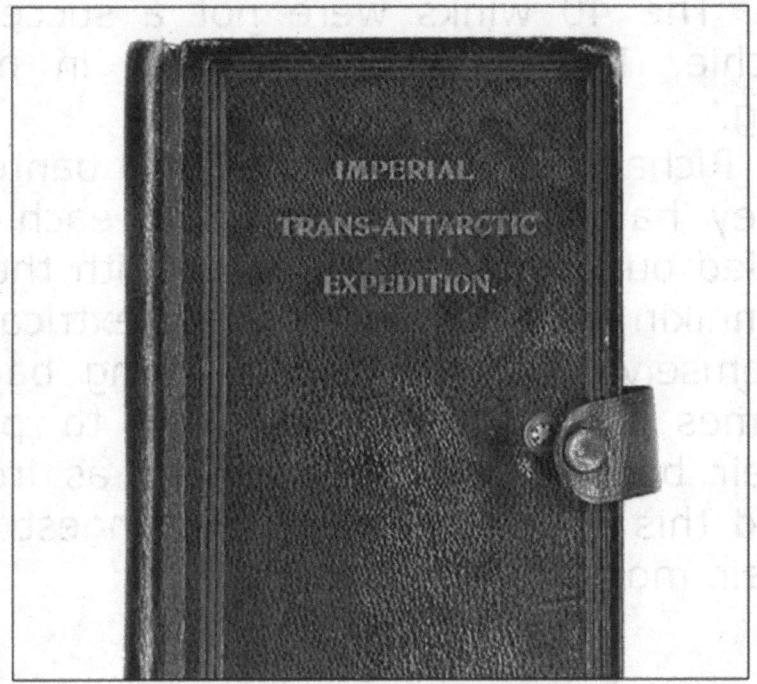

The ITAE diary issued to Richards and others on arrival at McMurdo Sound.

Hayward writes up his diary, and then he often tries to doze off again. He pulls the sleeping bag flap over his head and Richards hears his muffled voice.

"I'm surprised how comfy and warm it is. Just going to have another 40 winks, while I have the opportunity."

Ten minutes later Hayward is sitting up and he notices Richards is looking at him.

"The 40 winks were not a success Richie. There is no sleep left in my bag."

Richards smiles at Hayward's banter. They have cigarettes and one each is doled out, which they savour with their pannikin of tea. After they extricate themselves out of their sleeping bags comes the morning struggle; to put their boots on. They are hard as iron and this operation takes the longest of their morning activities.

***

Snow patters on the tent and the wind hisses. A mild blizzard is blowing one morning but Richards experiences a great sense of comfort in his sleeping bag. A jet of steam comes out of the sleeping bag opening as he breathes, as it does for Hayward and Ninnis.

Later on, the three men are sitting up in their sleeping bags. In their hands they clasp a pannikin of hoosh, so it does not lose heat quickly, and their hands become nicely warmed. A biscuit is broken into the hoosh, after first cracking it up with their teeth, and the first spoonful of hoosh gives them a delicious warm glow right through their body. A pannikin of tea follows, which is the end of the meal, but they are nicely warmed up. The only inconvenience is that the steam of the cooker condenses as tiny snow on the inside walls and comes down as a miniature snowstorm all over them when the tent walls are touched.

Hayward knows they will not be able to travel in the blizzard: "Nothing to do but remain in our bags and await the God of Blizzard's orders."

Richards smiles again at the Englishman's choice of words, and even more as he goes on talking. Hayward is keen to make a move as soon as possible: "That breakfast was very good. By Jingo, a man feels good after his pannikin of hoosh and tea. He is ready to push Mount Erebus over."

Their tent companion Ninnis is finding little pleasure in the work: "To me this is a hard life, to say nothing else. Sledging I've come to the conclusion is no joke. I began to wish the sledge in Kingdom Come."

Hayward ignores Ninnis' comment and starts writing diary notes to his

Ethel again, whereas Richards thinks of the girl on the train, her ringlets, her freckles, her strawberry-red lips, and he wishes he had her address.

The snow eases. Their wet socks from the previous day had been hung to dry, or at least to lose some of their moisture, but they are now frozen and as stiff as a board. To put them on requires beating and bending and tugging, all of which takes time. If they put their wet socks in their sleeping bags, they would stay soft but wet, an absolute horror to put on that way in the morning.

Then they roll up their sleeping bags and sit on these while wrestling with their boots, pushing and pulling until their feet are completely inside. Their boots are wet and freeze overnight, so they must be shaped carefully when they are put down for the night, so it is easier to get the tips of their toes inside the opening in the morning.

When they shake the side of the tent, down comes a shower of frost rime which has formed during the night, from their breathing and from the cooking. Some of the rime falls down their necks and they often start the day with a cold damp collar and jersey.

The middleclass Englishman Hayward comes out with another phrase new to Richards: "Such a ducky life is it not Richie?"

To which Richards replies: "Very different to being at home."

***

Richards, with Hayward and Ninnis, and along with Cope, Stevens and Hooke, haul their sledges up the wall of the Ross Ice Shelf. They are then on the Great Ice Barrier where the land ahead stretches in an unbroken horizontal line. An immense arc where there is nothing but a level snow-carpet below and – on this day – a cloudless sky above.

Richards is stunned by the scene, as well as by the solitude, the absolute silence. He sees an immense snow plain spreading southward, emanating out from the vast wall of the ice shelf.

"I heard Smithy describe the Barrier. He said it looks like land bediamonded by the sun, not that I knew what he meant until now. He's right. It looks like the surface is covered with diamonds."

Hayward is also taken in by the emptiness of the Barrier: "There's not a sound. What a place to think quietly."

"It will probably change when the wind blows," replies Richards. "I guess this snow plain goes all the way out to the Beardmore Glacier."

On most days they stop every half-hour for a three-minute rest, and after five hours' pulling the leader – at this time it is Cope who is in charge of the six men – calls out "Luncho". Up go the two tents where they have their lunch of tea, biscuits and chocolate. Their afternoon hauling usually goes on for another five hours.

Richards tells his fellow Australian Hooke that some of the party are feeling the effects of the sun and wind on their lips and face: "Especially those from the old country," he says.

For Richards, he is starting to enjoy the hauling, although sledging leaves no time for exalted thoughts. When he is pulling, he is uncomfortably hot. When he is resting, he is uncomfortably cold. And he is always hungry. However, he finds his fitness is improving day by day, and he finds solace as he trudges along, thinking his own thoughts. He has little else to do but to keep half an eye on the undulations on the frozen surface he is on, to avoid slipping badly or falling over. He finds his thoughts go in curious cycles. At times he simply meditates. However, when there is a feature ahead, such as a depot of stores others have put down, or a snow cairn, he makes guesses as to the number of paces away the feature is and starts counting. Then, for some reason – and Richards has no idea why – he finds he mechanically continues counting even after he has passed the feature.

In the evenings, the men tell each other of any ailments.

"My rupture is a bit painful tonight Vic," says Richards.

"You have not mentioned it before. How did it happen?" asks Hayward.

"In a football game back home in the last season. The doctors told me to use a truss, but no one knows I have it."

"It could be serious down here, if things go badly Richie."

"I know. Foolish to conceal it but I wanted to be here. How are you feeling?"

"I've had a piece of rotten luck to-day. When one of the sledges was stuck in the loose snow I got hold of the thing and gave a terrific wrench to get it out. The bally thing didn't budge, and I strained my back pretty badly. It has been very painful hauling."

***

In mid-February four teams are hauling provisions onto the Barrier. Mackintosh's team of he, Spencer-Smith and Wild, Joyce's team with he, Gaze and Jack, the team of Richards, Hayward and Ninnis, and the team led by Cope, with he, Hooke and Stevens. The latter two teams are still travelling together.

Men within each team live in harmony with each other, and there is no outward antagonism or conflict within any of the teams, at this early stage of the sledge hauling program. And, it is much the same in the relationship between the teams. For example, Mackintosh, Spencer-Smith and Wild find the surface much better on the Barrier than on the sea-ice and they even challenge Joyce's team to a race to Minna Bluff.

Spencer-Smith adds to the friendly rivalry by writing facetious messages in the snow, for Joyce's party to read:

BUCK UP. SHIP WILL CATCH YOU UP YOU

CRIPPLES.

And Wild adds by way of encouragement:

PUB AHEAD

Richards, Hayward and Ninnis enjoy each other's company, but there is frustration and anger at times in their relationship with the other team travelling with them; that of Cope, Stevens and Hooke.

"Slow progress," moans Hayward one evening. "It's is all because of Tanglefoot. That's what I shall call him, Tanglefoot, owing to his acrobatic feats when trying to retain his equilibrium."

Once again Richards is entertained by Haywards choice of words.

"And the other," continues Hayward, "I hereby name Skis and Sparrow Knees, owing to the decided affection his knees show for one another."

Richards, and Ninnis, start laughing at Hayward's mocking nicknames, who they believe refer to Stevens and Hooke.

"I know Vic," says Richards. "Progress is unsatisfactory. It is the amount of time they are taking over meal stops, and their slow rate of pulling."

Hayward in not happy: "The three of them just potter about, having spells for breathers and nibbles whenever they like. Today for instance we spent an hour and a half over the midday meal."

After another slow day of hauling, Hayward is even more disenchanted with the team of Cope, Stevens and Hooke. While putting up the tents, he suddenly loses his temper and starts yelling at Stevens and Hooke in particular.

"You men are just not pulling your weight. This is not a bally afternoon tea party. You have no experience of cold weather travel and are moreover hopelessly inefficient and incapable of even pulling your pound."

Stevens and Hooke ignore Hayward, but he continues haranguing them.

"Humbugs. That is what I see you as. The biggest messrs humbugs that it has been my misfortune to be up against. Don't you realize that we have a duty to perform and hard work in front of us?"

An hour later, after a meal of pemmican, Hayward sits with Richards and Ninnis in their tent, and they are surprised to be visited by Cope, Stevens and Hooke. But the visitors do nothing to reduce the disharmony when they bring in copious amounts of snow on their boots. Plus, when Stevens starts pouring out some tea from a thermos Cope drops his pannikin of tea all over Richards, and Hooke spills his over Hayward. The meeting is about to dissolve into a shouting match, but wise heads prevail, and peace and order is eventually restored.

However, Hayward continues to be agitated by the efforts of Cope, Stevens and Hooke. One morning, when there is a mild blizzard blowing, the three men refuse to march so Hayward goes over to their tent. When he returns to Richards and Ninnis, he explains how annoyed he is, in more turns of phrase that Richards finds most engaging.

"I cannot convince them that this light wind blowing and the small quantity of snow falling do not constitute a blizzard. And another factor contributing to my sense of discontent is that a man gets stale and loses his keenness, lying in his bag so long. I feel fresh and fit as the proverbial daisy on the march, whereas now I feel cramped and still all over."

To take his mind off the other tent, Hayward opens his diary.

"Here is something I do have to look forward to. I wrote this the other day, one of the champagne suppers Ethel and I will enjoy when I return. Listen to this. This is one menu I have drawn up. Real turtle soup, thick. Braised gosling and red currant Jelly. Pigeon pie. A pudding of beef, steak, lark and oyster. Toasted Cheshire cheese and black coffee."

"That's enough Vic," cries out Richards. "Enough about food. This sledging is a hungry and starving game."

***

Richards' team and Cope's team have dropped another load of provisions about 40 miles onto the Barrier, and are heading back towards Hut Point, but sledging and camping conditions have started to deteriorate during February. The sun now drops out of sight at night and the temperature then falls markedly.

Richards, Hayward and Ninnis lie in their sleeping bags.

"Having just finished our hoosh and tea I am just beginning to feel comparatively warm once more," says Hayward. "I have brought with me on this trip my old favourite Lorna Doone and I am about to have a rasp of it. Did you ever read it Rich? Aub?"

Richards and Ninnis shake their heads.

"I have an idea that I got it for Ethel somehow, but she said she could not tackle it. When I get back, I am going to insist upon her reading it. If she defies me, I will read it to her."

"Do you have a picture of this Ethel?" asks Richards.

Hayward holds up his diary, and Richards and Ninnis see a portrait photograph attached to the flyleaf. Ethyl is a young and very attractive woman, a vision beyond the wildest dreams for two young men in the frozen wastes of the Antarctic. They stare at the picture for a while but say nothing.

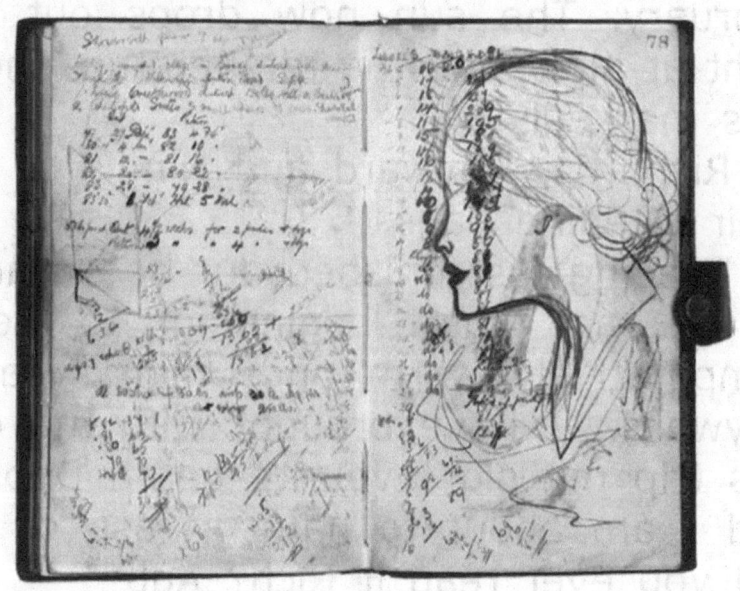

Extract from Hayward's diary, courtesy of Peter Hayward and the National Maritime Museum, Greenwich, London.

Ninnis changes the topic: "It's going to be very cold tonight. The temperature has now dropped to 50 degrees below freezing."

"My God," says Hayward. "That is probably why I am having a desperate time trying to get comfortable in my bag. A week ago, camping out here was pleasant. Now, every breath I takes condenses in the atmosphere of the tent and makes everything damp. Then it all freezes up."

"Not a lot we can do about it Vic," replies Richards. "When I came to take my boots off today my socks were frozen hard to the boots. It was hard to get them out of the boots without damaging them."

"Change your footwear Richie. Boots freeze as hard as boards and are very cold. Wear the finneskoe, like I do all the time. They are made from reindeer-skin with the fur on the outside and perfect for these conditions."

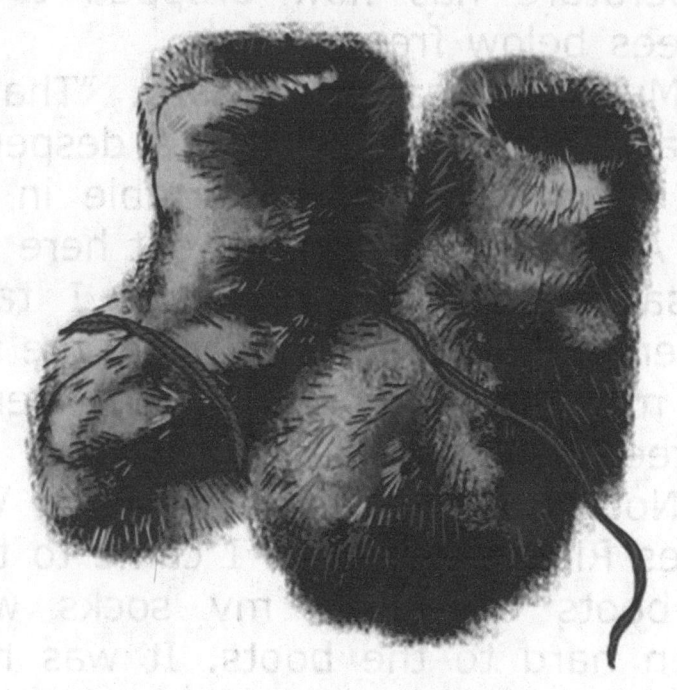

Finneskoe boots.

Even after a couple of weeks of sledging Richards is not sure what is more comfortable; to have a beard or not. Hayward knows exactly what he likes, and that is no beard. When they left the ship, he had his hair and beard closely clipped and he keeps taking snips of his beard every couple of days to keep it short. He tells Richards: "I find my face gets in a beastly mess if I have one. It freezes up and icicles form on it."

To keep his head warm Richards always wears a hat but Hayward never wears one. He knows he has no great protection from the elements, but he does not find it to be particularly cold when he is on the march. "Just being pragmatic I suppose Richie," he says, "as little things, like swollen cheeks and stiff necks, are simply part of the game. Without them to contend with I would almost feel out of place."

Richards, Hayward and Ninnis are comfortable in the tent as they place their sleeping bags close together, which give them the benefit of their combined warmth. But with temperatures always below zero, they must sleep with their heads inside their sleeping bags, without any fresh air to speak. They find it impossible to sleep with their heads exposed to the cold. One night, Richards and Ninnis are woken up by Hayward. He is inside his bag, yelling and shouting, and thrashing about wildly. Richards and Ninnis undo the toggles on his bag and Hayward springs out, which makes the other two collapse with laughter.

"Just like a Jack in the Box," is Ninnis' first comment.

"What is the problem Vic?" asks Richards.

"I was so cold I put my fur mitts on after I had tied up all the toggles of my bag. Somehow or other I dreamt during the night and I woke up suddenly. I could not imagine where I was, only that I was absolutely helpless and suffocating. I lashed out pretty freely and having fur mitts on I could feel nothing."

Richards smiles. "You should have heard your language. It almost made me blush."

CHAPTER 6
Ten men stranded

Cape Evans hut.

By the end of February, 'summer' in the Antarctic is ending. Richards' first season's sledging is complete. There are still men out on the Barrier laying depots – including Mackintosh, Joyce, Wild and Hayward – but Richards is with Spencer-Smith and others at the *Discovery* Hut at Hut Point. There is no sea-ice around the base of McMurdo Sound in late February, so these men expect the *Aurora* to arrive shortly and take them 13 miles north, to the hut at Cape Evans.

Richards and Spencer-Smith are sitting on packing cases, close to the blubber stove inside the hut, with two of the dogs. Richards bear-hugs one of them. "I presume Mack will bring the rest of the dogs in when he returns."

"Yes," replies Spencer-Smith. "He has nine or more out with him. See this one? Towser. Lovely dog, but Mack did not want him. He thought he slackened off when his name was yelled out."

"He's a great fat hulking animal."

"A fool Richie, and a great nuisance. He is always getting tied up in his harness, and that meant we had to keep stopping the sledge. We would give him a good beating as his crime was premeditated, we are sure."

"Lovely looking dog though, yellow and dashed with white."

"But a morose sulker, lazy and fat, and he always has to be hustled. We beat him again and again, but he never yelps or barks and Mack thinks he is quite hopeless for this task."

Richards fondles the ears of his dog. "What about this one? Gunner isn't it?"

"I sometimes call him Gunboat, but others call him Gunner. He is almost human. On one day he saw a fragment of dog biscuit on the track and grabbed at it. But he missed it, and for the next two or three minutes he sulked and refused to pull."

Richards smiles as Spencer-Smith goes on.

"Then, at another time, I thoughtlessly I let him see the biscuits I was carrying for lunch, and it was painful to see him look piteously at them."

"You are too soft Smithy."

"I am getting soft. I snapped a gold tooth clean off at supper time last night, and you know, the nearest dentist is in New Zealand. More worrying is that I'm a little strained on the left side intercostal; I hope it's not my heart. I shall have to be careful."

Richards and Spencer-Smith have little to do at the *Discovery* hut as they wait for some sign of the *Aurora,* and the bleak conditions inside force them to lie in their sleeping bags for extended periods. It is so cold they cannot even hold a pencil. They do manage to shovel out a few tons of ice and snow from the doorway of the hut, as until then they had to enter the hut through a window.

Richards is intrigued by the *Discovery* hut. "This is an interesting building. It's just a shed really, but it looks like it comes from Australia, with a veranda on three sides."

"It is from Australia Richie. Scott put it up fifteen years ago, but I think it was prefabricated in Sydney."

"Hardly a hut."

"You know Richie," muses Spencer-Smith, "people at home are just finishing their after-church supper. One wonders if they're thinking of us at all."

Richards rarely thinks of home, or of his family and old friends. He is completely embroiled in his new living conditions which are so foreign to those back in Australia, and with his newfound friends. He is quite content with the hand he has been dealt in the Antarctic.

***

In early March Richards, Spencer-Smith, Stevens, Gaze, Ninnis and Hooke are picked up from the *Discovery* hut by the *Aurora* and taken to Cape Evans. The first four – Richards, Spencer-Smith, Stevens and Gaze – move into the Cape Evans hut but the other two men choose to live on the ship.

There are still two teams out on the Barrier. One team consists of Hayward, Cope and Jack and they are stocking depots close to the edge of the Barrier. The other team is that of Mackintosh, Joyce and Wild, the three navy men, with the majority of the dogs. They are a considerable distance onto the Barrier, where they intend to put down a depot about 150 miles to the south from Hut Point. This is being done just in case Shackleton does come across the continent early; that is at in the end of this summer, in March 1915.

After dropping their last depot provisions, Hayward, Cope and Jack struggle back towards the *Discovery* hut. The discomfort of forcing themselves into a frozen sleeping bag at night makes the three men wonder if it would be better to keep marching. They do not look forward to turning in at night with any degree of pleasure. The lateness of the season – it is now early March – and the suddenness with which the cold weather has set in renders their sleeping bags practically uninhabitable. It is as much as they can do to get into them, as they are frozen hard.

When they reach the *Discovery* hut, they find nobody there, but a letter from Stenhouse which explains that two days previously the *Aurora* had picked up Richards, Spencer-Smith and others and taken them all back to Cape Evans. They had missed the *Aurora* by just two days. The ship has left some stores at Hut Point, for which tobacco is the most prized item but other articles like soap and towels are of no interest. They have not washed for seven weeks and are not going to start now. Tins of corned beef and sardines have been left for them also, but there is no opener to open them with, and their fingertips are so badly sore through frostbite they cannot open them with their fingers.

They expect Mackintosh, Joyce and Wild, who are still out on the Barrier, to join them within a few weeks. Then, they anticipate waiting at Hut Point for up to three months, that is until mid-winter, before the sea-ice freezes sufficiently to allow all of them to walk to Cape Evans.

***

Mackintosh, Joyce and Wild had reached the location for the laying of their most southerly depot, about 150 miles south of the huts, on February 20. They had made twelve miles on the previous day, and their reward, as promised by Mackintosh was as sip of alcohol.

"If we do 12 miles on any one day, there is a peg of brandy out of the medical comforts for all of us", he told Joyce and Wild. This was a cause for celebration for two of them, but not for Joyce, because he set fire to his brandy when he was trying to warm it.

As soon as breakfast is over the next morning, Joyce and Wild go off with a light sledge and the dogs to lay out the cairns and flags to provide direction to the depot. They spend a few days building up the depot itself, to about 10 feet high with a 15 feet pole, believing that it can be seen from about 12 miles on a clear day. They also put up cairns every mile, for five miles, to the east and west, all with flags and directions to reach the depot.

Mackintosh remains at the tent to take angles and fix their position with the theodolite. The temperature is very low and handling the theodolite is a difficult task as bare fingers must be used. The theodolite's arc and view become frozen over with the moisture from Mackintosh's breath. At times his whiskers freeze to the metal while he is taking a sight.

On February 24 Mackintosh, Joyce and Wild set off for Hut Point, 150 miles to the north, but very quickly, the condition of the dogs starts to concern them. The dogs are hungry, and they start to eat their harnesses, or any leather straps that are lying around. The men can give them nothing beyond their allowance of three biscuits each, as they are on bare rations themselves.

Then, they are held up by a blizzard, so they can do nothing but lie in their sleeping bags and wait. On almost every day Mackintosh writes diary notes sitting up in his bag, while the other two are usually snoring peacefully alongside him. Then he lies down, toggles up, and courts sleep. Sleep eventually comes, after he has let his mind wander over his entire life, past, present and future. At times, the three of them just lie there, talking over all kinds of subjects, or they sleep.

Their waking time during a blizzard, when there is enough light, is principally occupied by reading. They share their books; which include *Riddle of the Sands* by Erskine Childers and *Real's Soldiers of Fortune* by Richard Harding Davis. They must lie down in their sleeping bag when they read, so their upper body does not get cold. They also have to hold the book as close as possible to inside the sleeping bag, so their hands don't get chilled. While they read sleep often comes and the book falls into the sleeping bag as they doze off. At one time Wild decides to have his weekly clean of the pots and pans.

Blizzards rarely hold them up for more than a day. They do not need to travel at night, because the lower air temperatures and the harder snow allows them to sledge on the harder surface by day. Day travel also protects them from the ravages of the cold. However, the 150-mile trek back to Hut Point is an extremely difficult undertaking for Mackintosh, Joyce and Wild. By late-February, the refuge of their sleeping bags is not enough to keep out the cold and Wild even attempts to write up his daily log with his mitts on. Mackintosh's ears and fingers are now continually festering, Joyce's fingers are 'going' frequently, and Wild's nose is badly affected, as are his toes.

"When I woke this morning, I saw you rubbing your feet Wild," says Mackintosh.

"I was trying to bring my big toe around. It had 'gone'."

But Wild somehow maintains his cheery outlook: "It's the left foot now, presently it may have been the right. I've had scarcely any feeling in them for the past 24 hours."

"Let me have a look at them Tubby," says Joyce, who takes both of Wild's stockinged feet and places them under his own jacket to give them a strong rub.

"They are cold," he says.

Joyce peels off Wild's socks and sees the feet are black and blue like a bruise. Joyce smears them all over with some Vaseline and bandages them up. Mackintosh admires Wild's toughness: "You are as plucky as any Britisher Wild. How are your feet Joyce?"

"The only time I feel cold is when I have been without hoosh for some time."

And Joyce has concerns for Mackintosh: "Sir, what about you? How is your eye?"

"Painful Joyce. Very painful."

"Maybe you should never have left the ship Sir."

"All of us bear marks of our tramp. I think Wild takes first place. His nose is a picture for Punch to be jealous of. Joyce you have a good nose and many minor sores on your face. My jaw is swollen from the frost-bite I got on my cheek, and I also have a bit of nose."

But Mackintosh takes some solace in a glorious sunset.

"Did you see those golden colours illuminating the sky and the moon before? Casting gorgeous rays in combination with the more vivid one from the dipping sun. If all was as beautiful as the scene, we could consider ourselves in some paradise. But to come down to our position it's more like a cold hell!"

Under increasingly harsh conditions, these three Navy men, the officer Mackintosh and the two ex-Petty Officers in Joyce and Wild, maintain kind thoughts towards each other. Mackintosh writes up a private diary note at this time, where he states that Wild is a sterling sledging companion, a man who sleeps like a top, a remarkable little fellow who is always merry and bright. He notes that as soon as Wild lays down to sleep he starts snoring. Mackintosh sees Joyce as quite a different character to Wild, a man who is quite alright while humoured and then he is willing to do anything for anyone, but he has no stability. To Mackintosh, Joyce is fine while all is going well, but as a man he is not very resilient and feels the cold very easily, but he always sticks it out.

***

Life is pleasant for Richards at Cape Evans. He, Spencer-Smith, Gaze and Stevens, all sleep in the hut and carry out scientific work. The four men join the crew and others eating meals on the ship and enjoying the entertainment on board. The crew of the *Aurora* and others – like Ninnis and Hooke – eat and sleep on the ship.

A small supply of stores is unloaded for the four men in the hut; some butter, sugar, medical, Bovril rations and dog pemmican as there are five dogs at the hut. A limited stock of sledging stores is unloaded and stacked outside the hut. Only a little coke for their stove is issued, now and again, and similarly, rations of tobacco, cigarettes and liquor are only made from the ship on a weekly basis. Important sledging equipment, such as tents, reindeer sleeping bags and sledges remain on the ship.

Whereas the *Discovery* hut at Hut Point is nothing more than an empty shed, the hut at Cape Evans is far more substantial. It has Ruberoid on the roof, floor, walls and ceiling for insulation, plus additional insulation of finely shredded seaweed known as Gibson quilting on the walls. There is lighting, by acetylene gas, and heating from a coal-burning stove. The centre of the hut has a large table, and by the walls there are bunk beds, with separate sleeping areas and there is even a darkroom for photography, plus worktables for scientific equipment. Dusty windows bring in some light and the hut is littered with old pitchers, crockery, tins and crates of food, and many personal items like socks, fur boots, blankets, sleeping bags and books, all left by Scott's party.

Cape Evans had become the default winter berth for the *Aurora,* after Stenhouse failed to find more suitable winter mooring, at other nearby locations. She is iced in, near the Cape Evans hut, but tied up to the shore which is only 30-40 yards away. The sea-ice is sometimes firm enough for people to walk freely on it, whereas at other times a boat is used to ferry people and provisions between the ship and the shore. The ship is firmly attached, with her bows to the sea and with seven steel hawsers attached to two huge anchors which are iced into the shore. Holes had been dug for the anchors and water poured in, which became like concrete. Every now and again the crew equalise the tensions on the hawsers on the stern.

Like Richards, Spencer-Smith enjoys living in the hut, and these two men enjoy each other's company, having a lot in common; a University education, religion and sport.

"Richie, this stay is becoming noteworthy for a series of pleasant dreams of home. Woodbridge, Cambridge, Edinburgh. I had the best sleep of the trip last night. Thoroughly warm and comfy all night."

Instrument box outside the hut at Cape Evans.

Richards sets up a scientific program and at specific times he goes outside to take meteorological readings from instruments on the hillside around the hut. Sometimes as he dashes from the hut door to the hillside the wind catches him and sweeps his feet away, sending him flying through the ice and the snow. On very windy days he is blown over several times before he reaches the rubble slopes where the instruments are located. The others know how cold it is for Richards in handling and resetting the instruments, but as Richards is the youngest, it is accepted that he should be the most energetic of the 'science 'men.

***

"What is this place you come from Richie, Long Gully?" enquires Spencer-Smith one evening.

"It's a small place, so our community life is very close. At night families visit each other and sing around the piano, very satisfying for everyone, and most people are very religious."

"What denomination?"

"Baptist and Methodist.

Richards tries to give Spencer-Smith some inkling as to his childhood in Australia.

"Long Gully is not too far away from the bush and when I was a boy we would we would go there at weekends and cut down wattle trees, make sticks as guns and bows and arrows and pretend we were cowboys and Indians or soldiers in the recently concluded Boar War. We threw slag from the local mines at each other, which exploded with a little grey cloud. When I turned thirteen, I started to get interested in minerals, so I did a bit of geology on the muck heaps."

"You lived in a mining area?"

"Yes. I used to search the slag heaps for mica, glaciers, jasper, calcimine and other minerals. Many of the miners are from your old country, Cornwall. Wherever you go you hear the Cornish accent, it is quite common, as are the Cornish pasties."

Spencer-Smith is enthralled as Richards' continues describing his upbringing, so foreign to his own.

"I went to a few schools before I was thirteen and then I went to what we call a secondary school in Bendigo, where I did courses that allowed me to enter University. I lived at home and walked to school every day, about three miles, a fine method of development for a child. My knees and legs are the strongest part of my body. Interestingly, there is a tram line between Bendigo and Long Gully, a steam tram, but the engine power is insufficient to take the tram up a small hill. The occupants have to disembark and walk up the hill. A horse drawn cab follows the tram and offers rides to people walking. We could never afford to take the tram."

Spencer-Smith smiles.

"Very different to me Richie. I was born in Streatham, London, but when I was thirteen, I was sent to a boy's boarding school, Woodbridge in Suffolk. About a hundred miles northeast of London. I loved my time there, as I was very involved in sport, especially cricket."

Richards goes over to his bunk and picks up his *magazine* NATURE.

"That's why I brought this to read Smithy. This is the only book I brought from Australia because there is a wonderful article on why a cricket ball swings. I became fascinated by the 'googly' and I think an Englishman named Bosanquet invented it. I tried to work out the physics of it, a ball that looked like it should turn one direction when it hit the pitch, but it would move in the opposite direction."

Spencer-Smith remembers more of his days at Woodbridge.

"In one cricket game, I scored not out 9, batting with a Mister WH Balgarnie who I believe was the inspiration for the character Mr Chips in James Hilton's book Goodbye, Mr. Chips."

Richards cannot better that story: "At sixteen I went to Melbourne University. What about you Smithy, when did you go to University?"

"About the same age. At Queens in Cambridge I was the founding editor of the student magazine. Someone wrote an article that I played an extremely useful spoiling game of football, which I don't think is any compliment."

Richards reminisces: "At my teacher training college in Melbourne they gave us an allowance of twelve pounds a year, which we all managed to exist on, as we had our board and washing done. It was amazing how we would spend the one pound a month. We would go down to the city for a bit of a binge, to a wine shop and have a Madera there, our favourite tipple. Or walk through the Exhibition Gardens to the Melbourne Cricket Ground to see a football match or a game of cricket. It cost sixpence to get in. Now and again we would go to the theatre, where there would be men called 'packers', who would come along and pack you in like sardines to get one or two more in a row. We had a good time there."

"After University I taught French and Mathematics, in Scotland," says Spencer-Smith. "Then in 1913 I was elected a Fellow of the Royal Historical Society and the following year submitted my application to join Shackleton's expedition as its chaplain and photographer. So here I am."

"Well Smithy, for me after University I taught at places you would not have heard of, one near Birchip in the Mallee in Victoria, then at a school in Gippsland, and from there I was sent to Shelbourne, near Bendigo, before ending up at the Ballarat Junior Technical School. There I rowed, played football – Australian football – with a Ballarat team and a bit of cricket too. But then I saw an advertisement in the paper for a Physicist in the Antarctic. So here I am too."

Spencer-Smith changes the topic.

"The cook said to come over later today to fetch a plum-duff."

Richards is bewildered: "A what? A plum duff? What is that?"

"A great British pudding Ritchie, you will love it."

"If not, I'll feed it to the dogs."

Spencer-Smith laughs. "The dogs are happy enough. Titis Oates' old horse stables are perfect for them."

Richards assumes that Mackintosh will be bringing all his dogs back.

"Well, we only have five, but remember that Mack has another dozen or so with him. When they get here, it will be bedlam."

At this time, mid-April, Richards and his three companions, Spencer-Smith, Stevens and Gaze, live and work at the Cape Evans hut, but they enjoy the facilities on the *Aurora* anchored just offshore. There are still six men – Mackintosh, Joyce, Hayward, Wild, Cope and Jack – at the *Discovery* hut. However, they must wait until June or at worst July, for the sea between Hut

Point and Cape Evans to be frozen solid before they can safely walk to Cape Evans.

***

"There goes the sun," says Richards.

On the twentieth of April the sun fails to rise above the horizon, but a soft twilight hangs over the land during the day. However, by early May much of the day is as black as the night. On the sixth of May the wind freshens in the afternoon, and by midnight a mild blizzard is blowing, but Richards is the only one in the hut to show some concern.

"I presume the ship is safe, tied up out there?" he says to Gaze, Stevens and Spencer-Smith.

"Well, the crew think so," replies Spencer-Smith.

That night, Spencer-Smith tells Richards he will take the midnight meteorological readings, and that he will wake Richards for the later readings. Richards is woken by Spencer-Smith at three, so he puts on his boots and coat and goes outside to take readings from the instrument boxes away from the hut. The moderate blizzard is still blowing, and as was usual, there are snow drifts about 20-30 feet high around the hut. The night is fairly clear, and it is a moonlight night.

As Richards leaves the door of the hut, he looks to his right down to the beach, expecting to see the tops of the masts of the ship above the snow drift. But there are no masts to be seen. He walks the 20 or so yards down to the water's edge to find an anchor in the sand with the hawsers and the cables broken. A second anchor is further down the beach, also with its cables snapped.

Anchor of the Aurora in the gravel beach at Cape Evans.

He rushes back inside the hut, and yells: "She's gone! The ship's gone!"

Spencer-Smith, Stevens and Gaze bolt upright in their bunks.

"What do you mean Richie? What ship has gone?" Gaze calls out.

"Our ship. The *Aurora*. It's not there."

The four men go outside and all they can see is open water. They are stunned, but quickly realise that the ice clamping the ship had been swept away by the blizzard, taking the *Aurora* with it.

"You now, all the men on the ship thought it was quite safe for the winter," says Spencer-Smith, who is very concerned. "What do we do now?"

"Wait," says Stevens. "With a day or two of reasonable weather she might be back."

The ship does not return. Whatever hopes they had for its reappearance are shattered when the worst blizzard they have experienced so far rages violently for the next three days. They now doubt whether the ship will come back before January in the following year.

The four men then discuss what they have on hand, and what they need to survive. Mattresses, rugs, books and cutlery had been taken ashore but they are wearing their only clothing, except for a few extra items in their bags. Apart from a small supply of sledging rations no stores of food have been landed from the *Aurora*. However, they locate additional sledging rations plus a stockpile of food on a hill to the east of the hut, that Scott from his *Terra Nova* Expedition had fortunately left behind. That expedition had been lavishly supplied and the men find boxes of Henry Tate cubed sugar, jams, flour, hops, tinned vegetables, tinned meat, even tins of cakes. After a reconnoitre they estimate they have general stores, flour and similar items to last 10 men for two years.

Supplies of Henry Tate sugar at Cape Evans.

They even find small quantities of luxury items; many Richards has never heard of.

"Look at these Richie," calls Spencer-Smith. "Huntley and Palmer cakes all sealed up in tin containers, and Fray Bentos preserved meats, and tins of Beach's jams. Beautiful."

They have almost no coal for the stove, but they know seal blubber will work as fuel, and they can kill seals for additional food, providing them with fresh meat.

"You know," says Spencer-Smith, "worst of all; I don't think there is any tobacco in the hut."

Stevens thinks of Mackintosh: "I wonder what Mack will say when he gets here?"

***

"What are those bloody dogs barking at?" Richards calls out.

He pulls on his coat and wanders outside into the gloom of a moonlit night to yell at the dogs.

"Quiet Oscar, Towser!"

The dogs go quiet. Richards turns to go back inside but then he hears voices. It is the six men who were at the *Discovery* hut.

"Bloody hell," exclaims Joyce as he enters the Cape Evans hut, "I can't see." He fumbles in his coat pocket for his snow goggles. "That acetylene light is too strong."

Richards, Spencer-Smith, Stevens and Gaze stare at Mackintosh, Joyce, Wild, Hayward, Cope and Jack. Richards is blunt: "You look like scavengers."

"Thank God you are all safe," says Spencer-Smith. "You are so dirty looking and hairy."

Wild has more practical things on his mind: "A smoke. I need a smoke. We ran out of tobacco at Hut Point."

"We don't have any Tubby," says Richards. "The ship was blown away."

The six new arrivals stare at Richards, who continues: "It was a month ago. A bad blizzard came up and the ship was taken out of the Sound. It took six wire hawsers and a heavy chain cable with her and she's not been seen or heard of since."

No one speaks. Mackintosh digests the news: "We can only hope for the best, that she has been blown clear of the ice-pack and made her way to Hobart."

The crisis immediately hits home for Joyce. "Which means we won't see her till next January."

"But," replies Mackintosh, "we are ten men who can still relieve Shackleton at the Beardmore Glacier."

Worrywart Joyce is not happy: "Without any equipment to speak of. And all my clothes are on the ship. What do I have? A signet shirt, my drawers, two pairs of socks, one pair of finneskoe, and a cardigan."

Wild also realises the predicament they are in, and that the security, comfort and conditions he was looking forward to on the *Aurora* are no longer there.

"So, we are only a little better off than we were at Hut Point. I suppose we'll get over it alright."

"What do you mean Tubby?" says Hayward. "This hut is a palace compared to Hut Point."

Richards suddenly realises the six arrivals have no dogs with them: "Where are your dogs Mack?" he asks.

Joyce does not wait for Mackintosh to answer: "Dead Richie," he blurts out. "Every damn one of them. They died in the snow."

Richards can feel the tension between Joyce and Mackintosh. Both of Mackintosh's decisions – to use the dogs immediately and to not unload stores and send the ship back to Australia for the winter – have turned out to be wrong, and possibly calamitous.

CHAPTER 7

Winter at the Cape Evans hut

A day after his arrival at the Cape Evans hut from Hut Point Mackintosh calls a meeting, to give an outline of the situation. The ten men, Mackintosh, Joyce, Wild, Spencer-Smith, Hayward, Gaze, Jack, Cope, Stevens and Richards sit around the table in the hut.

"We are surprised to see you here, so early in June," says Richards. "We kept noticing the changing sea-ice conditions. A water stretch had been opening up consistently between here and Hut Point during blizzards and it would have been a real disaster if that had happened when you were crossing."

"It was a risk Richie," says Joyce, "but the Skipper and I went north and found the ice bearable, so we decided to trek. The moon shone brightly but we hadn't been trekking more than an hour when it became obscured, and we ended up in churned up ice. We were lucky not to fall through."

Later that day, Richards is outside the hut with Wild.

"You know Rich, he's daft than man, the Skipper," says Wild. "When we first got to Hut Point, he had some daft ideas about getting back here, straight away. One was, that he wanted to start back himself or with one companion and try to walk back taking nothing with them. So, we said what if a blizzard comes on? And his crazy reply was they would lie down and cover themselves with their Burberrys until it's over. We didn't know what he meant."

"Joyce told me about an incident at Hut Point," says Richards, "when you fell through a seal hole which was snow covered. He said you were as stiff as a board before you got to the hut which was only 150 yards away."

"Righto," says Wild. "After I got out, I made tracks back to the hut as fast as possible. I rattled as I walked, my clothes were that stiff, and of course I had no other clothes, so it wasn't much of a joke. There were only three sleeping bags at the hut, and the

Skipper and I were sharing one. He didn't even ask me if I would turn in to keep warm while my clothes were drying, but calmly turned in himself and went to sleep."

Wild shakes his head: "But I knew the Skipper had a combination suit so I asked him for a loan of it, till mine were dry, but he wouldn't lend it to me, said it was frozen. Then Joycey and I are out cleaning the sledges the next day and the combination suit falls out of the Skipper's bag, as dry as a bone."

Richards is appalled by Mackintosh's actions towards Wild.

***

At Cape Evans seals must be killed continually as their blubber is now the only source of fuel, and seal is virtually their only source of fresh meat. They manage to kill only a few penguins. On a day when Joyce, Richards and Wild are out searching for seals, Richards tries to find out more about the dogs.

"How come none of the dogs survived?" he asks Joyce.

"They were all fine, most of them anyway, for the first two weeks, and they should have gone back then. I had Mack to one side and tried to persuade him not to take the dogs any further south. They were feeling the effects of the hard sledging and weren't acclimatized."

Wild takes up the story. "They had no food. We could give them nothing beyond their allowance of three biscuits each. Then they started to eat their harness or any straps that were about. Shacks demolished all his harness, canvas, leather, brass and rivets. He was the best dog we had."

"One night I heard one of them bark," says Joyce, "so I went out to investigate. Major, feeling hungry, had dragged his way to my ski and eaten off the leather binding. Another dog had eaten all my harness, canvas and even rope."

"Then another blizzard hit us," says Wild, "and we lost a couple more days. Trekking was out of the question as the blizzard was a fury. We were by then on half rations ourselves, and nothing for the dogs. When it stopped blowing, I dug out them out, although I couldn't find them at first as they were completely buried. I had to take directions from the sledge mast. After an hour I had them out and I gave them extra biscuits as they all looked so thin. I fed them but they seemed very weak. My heart ached for them."

Joyce lays the blame entirely with Mackintosh: "I don't know how I refrained from giving Mack a bit of my mind then. I had to keep quiet as we had enough to think about before we got back to Hut Point."

"Did you put them down Joycey?"

"No. We just took them out of their harness, and they followed us for a while. Then they dig a hole in the snow and lie down, and that is to be their grave. Fortunately, they die a peaceful death as they go to sleep in the snow and unless something wakes them up, they stay there."

Wild starts to name each dog, and their deaths.

"Poor old Shacks fell out, we had to leave him. Then Nigger, the leader of the pack gave in, so I unharnessed him, his legs refusing to support him. Then, all the remaining dogs chucked their hands and we had only Pinky left. He had a good feed that night and then a busman's holiday riding on the sledge the next day, but a cold one with the temp about 20 below. Then he collapsed; our last dog, and I was more than sad about it."

Joyce is still angry. "It all could have been avoided, if Mack had shown some common sense early on."

Wild adds laconically: "I said we should call the place the Dead Dog Trail."

***

Richards is staring at a huge seal, only a few feet away. It is mid-winter, but the weather is reasonable, so Richards and Joyce are out in the dim twilight searching for seals. The only area they can find them is near a break in the sea-ice, at the edge of the shore. Richards swings his pick handle and gives the seal a whack on the nose, which stuns the animal and then Joyce immediately cuts its throat, and gushes of blood burst out from its arteries. He then runs a slit right up the body of the seal and quickly dips his bare hands inside the animal's stomach, to keep his hands from freezing. Joyce uses bare hands with the sealing knife, because with mitts on it is too dangerous; the knife can slip and cut his hands badly. The two men work together, with Joyce cutting long slits down the seal's body, and Richards using a cargo hook to pull up the blubber up in a strip. Joyce eases the blubber away from the seal's body as Richards pulls, creating a strip of blubber about six feet long.

"Lay it out on the ice," says Joyce. "It will freeze like a plank. We'll come out later and load the frozen planks onto a sledge. We'll cut it up with an axe back at the hut."

Richards looks around and sees clear white snow bespattered with blood, a regular battlefield. At first, he detested the job, but his tender instincts soon vanished. It was brutal, but their only method of procuring fuel and (fresh) food.

"Before we are finished, we need to cut out flesh from the middle section of the body. Let me tell you Rich, this seal meat will keep the scurvy down."

"Mack doesn't like it."

"I know Richie. And, already he's not up to the mark. He had some sort of skin disease when we were out before and I think it was probably scurvy manifesting itself."

"Smithy is the same. The two of them never eat fresh meat; they prefer tinned food or pemmican."

Inside the Cape Evans hut, Mackintosh and Spencer-Smith sip pannikins of tea as they sit together at the table. They enjoy each other's company.

"Joyce and Richards are out hunting seals now, but I can't do it anymore padre. It really is murder killing these innocent harmless brutes."

" I cannot do it either. They roll their eyes and start with fright when they see you. That is their only sign of objection, and then they open their mouths and give a swish with the tail."

"The only way I can justify it padre, for my conscience, is to look at it as a case of survival of the fittest. What I hated even more than the killing was that I couldn't clean myself afterwards. My clothes became 'blubbier' and 'blubbier'."

***

At Cape Evans, complete darkness sets in over the winter months from April to August. The ten men are stranded with very little equipment and almost no proper clothing. Mackintosh had intended to use *Aurora* as the party's main living quarters, so most of the shore party's personal gear, food, equipment and fuel were still aboard when the ship was taken away. However, life is not particularly unpleasant, or taxing.

There is an elementary wireless set in the hut, but Hooke had been unable to make it work while he was at Cape Evans. Hooke is now on the *Aurora*. Richards and Gaze try to make it operational so they can contact the ship, but their efforts are futile, and the men realise they will have no outside contact with anyone, until a relief ship arrives.

Mackintosh establishes a routine where he, Stevens, Richards, and Spencer-Smith have breakfast at 7a.m. and the others – Joyce, Hayward, Wild, Gaze, Jack and Cope – are called at

9a.m., and their breakfast is served. Then the table is cleared, the floor is swept, and the ordinary work of the day commences. They dig out sledging ration boxes, locate and repair old equipment, and kill seals and penguins. At 1p.m. they have what they call 'a counter lunch,' that is, cold food and cocoa. They work from 2p.m. till 5p.m. and dinner is at 7. The men then play games, such as Bobs, an abbreviated version of billiards played on an ordinary table, and cards after Spencer-Smith makes a pack of playing cards out of blank post cards. They read and write up diaries, impromptu sing-alongs provide entertainment and games of bridge entertain some of the men in the evenings. They turn in early, as they must economize fuel and light. Night-watches are kept by the scientists, who have the privilege of turning in during the day.

The search for seals takes up a great deal of their time, and when they are visible on the ice the men make every effort to kill as many as possible and store the blubber and the meat. Fresh water is obtained by digging out chunks of ice from a clean ice supply and sledging them to the hut, where a large container on the cooking range is kept filled with water.

Richards continues with his scientific experiments and observations. He constructs a dust counter for estimating the amount of dust in the air, and he also starts recording soundings and temperatures, observations on the rate of formation or dissolution of fresh-water ice in the sea and the rate of removal of ice from the ponds by evaporation.

Mackintosh has a bath in mid-June; his first wash for over four months and with his hair and whiskers cut, he feels he is gradually becoming civilised again. Hayward reveals his delight in being back in more pleasant living conditions than he had experienced at the *Discovery* hut and on the Barrier: "By Jingo, what a joy to sleep in something dry every night. I feel quite young again."

Hayward writes copious notes in his diary to his 'Ethel', with a list of some of the books he has read recently; books such as *The History of Henry*

Esmond by William Makepeace Thackeray, *The Mill on the Floss* by George Eliot, *It Is Never Too Late to Mend* by Charles Reade, *No.5 John Street* by Richard Whiteing, and many more. But he then tells her that he is never idle, and it would be wrong of her to think that, just because he has listed all these books.

June 22 is 'Christmas Day in winter' in the Antarctic and it is a day of celebration. They have a fine dinner, Christmas pudding and then play games, such as potato races, with tins of milk as potatoes and pin the tail on the donkey. Mackintosh proposes a toast to the King and to 'The Boss' (Shackleton).

The ten men finish their day of celebration singing shanties: 'Ranzo', 'Farewell, Spanish maidens', 'Grace Darling', 'Pull for the Shore', and other fragments of songs. Richards is captivated by the naval men – Mackintosh, Wild and Joyce – singing 'the Yankee Ship':

> *Oh blow me boys I loves to hear yer, Blow boys blow*
> *Oh blow me boys I loves to hear yer, Blow me bully boys blow.*

He finds he can even join in with the singing of the Drunken Sailor.

Oh what shall we do with a drunk-en sailor?
Oh what shall we do with a drunk-en sailor?
Oh what shall we do with a drunk-en sailor, ear-ly in the morn-ing?
Weigh-aye, up she ris-es, Oh-aye, up she ris-es, weigh-aye, up she ris-es, ear-ly in the morn-ing.

"What an oasis in the wilderness it would be if a case of tobacco had been landed," says Joyce towards the end of the day. "A pipe of the soothing weed makes all the world akin."

All the men smoked, usually pipes, and it was a major concern that they had no tobacco. They tried to improvise and make their own, using ingredients such as tea, coffee, dried mixed vegetable, sawdust, senna grass and different kinds of dirt, but nothing worked to their satisfaction.

For Hayward: "Being absolutely stumped for tobacco is the worst blow of all. I can remember my last puff, about two months ago. I was in the tent and I must have been three hours collecting every scrap of tobacco I could find amongst my personal gear. The net result after removing bits of biscuit, sleeping bag hair and whatever, was just about enough for one cigarette. However, I enjoyed it more than any gold tipped I ever smoked."

Wild smiles: "You can have some of my Hut Point Mixture."

"I've tried that," says Richards, "and it's a villainous concoction. What is in it?"

"Tea, coffee and sawdust."

"Have you noticed that only you can smoke that Tubby?" says Hayward. "I tried it as well and it just made me expectorate freely."

"Me too Vic," says Richards. "I was coughing and spitting up phlegm all the time."

Wild laughs, but Richards goes on: "We can always trail you over the sea-ice Tubby, by the black gobs that freely mark your track."

***

"What date do we start Skipper?" asks Wild.

"In just over two months, on the first of September."

It is near the end of June, and Mackintosh has all the men seated at the table in the centre of the hut. Their grimy fingers clasp hot pannikins of tea and they listen as Mackintosh outlines his plan of action for the following summer. He explains that three teams, each of three men, will be used to stock the depots for Shackleton. One person will remain behind for keeping the meteorological records and laying in a supply of meat and blubber.

Joyce agrees that one man should be left behind: "This man would be able to hand instructions to the ship when she returns and pilot a party to the Bluff to meet us."

Richards is taken back by Mackintosh's next statement: "And Richards will be the one to stay."

As much as he is a scientist, Richards has no desire to be left at the hut carrying out scientific work. Being a member of a sledging team has far more appeal. He was looking forward to the physical challenge of again hauling a sledge on the Barrier and sharing the arduous but exciting life with two companions in a tent. He wanted to be involved in putting down the more southerly depots for Shackleton. Fortunately for Richards, others do not agree with Mackintosh's plan, particularly Joyce.

"Sir, I object. Let's start with everyone helping at first and delay the decision on who should stay until the parties have had some practical work."

"Joyce could be right Skipper," says Hayward. "Richards is very healthy, and he may not be the best person to leave behind."

Mackintosh agrees to delay the decision on who should stay. (As it turns out, Gaze stays behind at first because of problems with his feet, but eventually it is Stevens who is left at Cape Evans.)

Mackintosh then tells the men he has worked out the calculations as to what is to be stored at each depot location. He stresses that stores to be left must be sufficient, not only for Shackleton's party but for themselves on their returning trek, enough to reach the next depot. He points out that one week's worth of provisions will be rationed to cover the 70 miles between depots. If men are delayed for any reason on their homeward journey, such as losing days because of a blizzard, and it takes longer than a week to cover the distance between depots, they have to go on reduced rations to make the food and fuel last until they make that next depot.

"The first step is for all the stores for the depots and that is about 4,000 pounds, have to be taken from here to Hut Point," he tells everyone. "That will take us about a month."

"We can use the five dogs we have to help as we will be skiing on the sea-ice," says Joyce.

"Correct Joyce. Stage two is to then take all the stores from Hut Point up onto the Barrier and set up a major depot about 70 miles out."

Joyce continues to flaunt his 'local' knowledge, and experience. "That will be at Minna Bluff," he tells everyone. "I estimate that will take us about three months Skipper. October, November and December."

Mackintosh agrees. "Yes. The Minna Bluff depot must be stocked with all the stores we need for the more southerly depots. There will be five of these depots which must be put down south of Minna Bluff depot. They will be at each latitude degree, and then a final one at Mount Hope at the Beardmore. Our journey from here to Mount Hope and back will be almost 800 miles."

Joyce knows Mackintosh is downplaying how far they will travel: "But the total distance we'll travel will be much more Sir. We'll have to make a number of trips out and back to fully stock the Bluff Depot. We will be covering something closer to 1500 miles I think."

Mackintosh concludes his talk: "So we start in early September, and I think we will be back here about the middle of March."

"A stupendous undertaking," exclaims Hayward.

"If accomplished will be almost a record of south polar travel," says Joyce.

Spencer-Smith turns to Richards: "It's a pretty big problem Richie. And there'll be ten very much played out men at the end of it, but, it's all in the game."

"It could be tough going for five months."

"Deo Vilente, we shall get through all right."

"God willing," adds Richards.

***

On a Sunday in early July, Mackintosh joins Spencer-Smith as the padre holds Holy Communion. The two men sit in the dark room where Spencer-Smith has set up as his chapel. He has even rigged up an altar, but Mackintosh is the only member of his 'congregation'.

These two men have now developed a close affinity with each other, as Mackintosh finds Spencer-Smith is the only man he can mention his inner thoughts to and discuss personal situations. He misses the services of another officer, someone who could be an intermediary with the men.

"My thoughts are always on the fate of the ship padre. They are so constant that I find myself dispirited, which I strive to fight against."

"But you do have a sterling lot of chaps here Skipper."

"I know. Joyce oversees the equipment and has undertaken to improvise clothes out of what canvas can be found here. Wild is working with him."

Wild is a favourite of Spencer-Smith: "He is such a cheerful, willing soul. Nothing ever worries or upsets him, and he is ever singing or making some joke or performing some amusing prank."

Mackintosh is pleased with all the Australians: "Richards has taken over the keeping of the meteorological log. He is a young Australian, a hard, conscientious worker, and I look forward to good results from his endeavours. Jack is his assistant, and Gaze, another Australian, is working in conjunction with Hayward."

All the men work on activities, to enable them to be ready to depart south in September. The two ex-Petty Officers Joyce and Wild, utilising their sewing skills developed over years in the navy, are making windproof canvas trousers and blouses, out of an old tent. They are very short on clothes but luckily, they find a pile of old underclothing in the hut. Footgear is another major problem, but more boots are made from canvas, and sets of fur boots are made too, by cutting up old sleeping bags and a horse rug.

An old pole tent left from Scott's 1910–1913 *Terra Nova* Expedition is found buried in the snow outside the hut and it is resurrected, which gives them the three tents they need. They have two of their own; a new conical tent and a pole tent, both of which had been used earlier in the year. They find two old primus stoves, which are repaired, and this gives them three working stoves, one for each team.

Joyce and Wild are working at the table in the centre of the hut.

"Oxford bags Ern, that what they look like," says Joyce as he holds up a roughly made pair of trousers.

"You know Joycey," says Wild, "I never thought a canvas tent could be turned into ten sets of trousers."

The ten men work well together. There are no animosities, just the occasional flare up, but nothing serious, where arguments are friendly and usually over trivial things, like the number of miles around the Australian coastline. They refer to a copy of a 1912 Encyclopaedia Britannica at the hut for answers. Arguments get quite heated, but personal relationships are astonishingly good.

Boxes of old sledging food, again left by Scott, are dug out from snow drifts around the hut, so they have adequate sledging food of pemmican, biscuits, etc.

Richards and Gaze are given the task of weighing and packing sledging rations into calico bags, and they follow the instructions provided by Joyce on the precise food allowance per day per man:

Pemmican	8oz.
Oatmeal	1 3/4oz.
Sugar	5 1/3oz.
Glaxo	2/3oz. (a dried milk powder)
Chocolate	1 1/4oz.
Tea	1/4oz.

Biscuit   1lb.

"Tubby and I have to make about 500 of these calico bags," Joyce tells Richards and Gaze. "All you have to do is weigh out the daily ration for three men and put it into one bag."

Richards understands the logic behind the rationing.

"So, seven bags will be the food allowance for a team of three men, to last those seven days, to travel from one depot to the next."

Joyce nods in agreement. (Neither man realizes how meaningful this weekly food allowance will become in the following year.)

***

August 22 is a very welcome date – as the sun reappears – and the men are buoyed by its return, even though some complain that the daylight now makes it difficult for them to sleep. They see the sun's rays peeping through over Mount Erebus and the light makes them blink.

A few days later, on a fine morning, some of the men go outside to look at the surrounding countryside. Seeing the colour of the land and sea outside seems so novel, but beautiful, after everything being obscured in darkness for so long. Then, later that same day, a veil of clouds slowly sweeps over, partially obscuring everything, and by 8p.m. the wind is blowing at 50mph and a snow drift is obliterating everything.

"From Paradise to Hades in a few hours," says Mackintosh.

In late August, just before they start sledging, the men try to clean themselves. Their Jaeger clothing and their Burberry's are run through with petrol, a task they find to be very cold and painful. They also endeavour to sponge themselves down as best they can. Wild sits in a tub of warm water.

"First wash for eight months for me," he calls out.

Cope, a botanist, is the 'medical officer' and he examines all the men.

"You are perfectly fit Skipper," he tells Mackintosh, "and most of the others are quite sound. Spencer-Smith worries me, as although he is perfectly sound in body and limb, he has an intermittent heart."

"He can go sledging?"

"Yes, but I told him if he feels any effects of his heart he is to turn back at the earliest possible moment."

Concerned that he may be the man left behind at Cape Evans, because of the truss for his rupture, Richards refuses to be examined. He tells Cope he is fully fit.

Shortly before setting off, Spencer-Smith writes a letter to his parents. Richards watches him: "What are you doing Smithy? There is nothing to write about. Not yet anyway."

"Writing to my mother and father Richie. Just a short note to say, 'au revoir' in case I should not come back, as there are some risks ahead."

Spencer-Smith's letter mentions there have been 'various misfortunes', meaning the loss of the *Aurora* and the death of most of their dogs, but they are now setting out for the next season's sledging. They will be working under 'rather precarious conditions'; with poor equipment, possibly too early in the year and with heavy loads. He explains how he and the others have had a 'pretty stiff time' but he has no regrets, except that he would have liked to have been with his mother and father 'during the horror of the war'. He goes on to tell his parents that if anything does happen to him, he will face it as cheerfully as he can, but he is 'sure & certain' of seeing them again. He concludes his letter saying: 'Goodbye for the moment'.

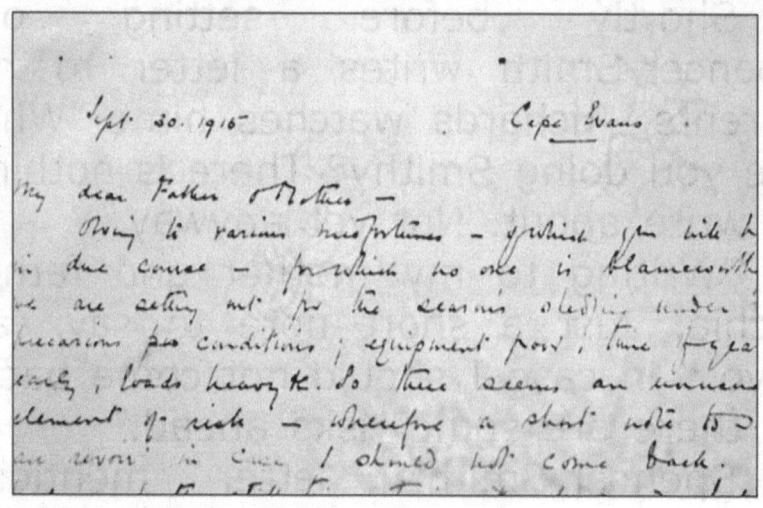

Spencer-Smith letter to his father and mother, courtesy of Debby Horsman, great-niece of AP Spencer Smith.

Over the winter months the ten stranded men have managed to produce makeshift clothes and boots for themselves and organize old sledging provisions into the required ration packs, in spite of major obstacles created by the loss of their ship.

It is now September and Richards' role as a scientist does not remerge. His sole task is to work with the others in man-hauling sledges laden with provisions, which will be used to stock the depots for Shackleton.

CHAPTER 8

Christmas day on the Great Ice Barrier

"Rouse out! Rouse out!" is the common call to the men to start a day after their breakfast and "Right-oh", would come any replies. To pull down their tents they clear snow blocks from the skirting, lift it up from the windward side so it blows out, shake off some of the icier lumps, and then fold it up. After packing the sledge, they look at each other's faces for frostbite. A dead-white nose tip or a white spot on a cheek are common signs and these are nursed back to life with the warmth of their bare hands.

On schedule, the new season of sledging started on September 1 of 1915. The first step was to take all the depot provisions from Cape Evans to the *Discovery* hut at Hut Point, and four of the five remaining dogs were used at this time to help pull the sledges. The dogs, Oscar, Towser, Gunner and

Con, (the fifth dog is pregnant), were employed because the route between the huts was over sea-ice, and on that sort of surface the men could normally ski. This meant they could work in harmony with the dogs, as their skiing speed was like the dog's normal rate of hauling; faster than a man's normal walking pace.

By early October, over a multitude of trips, all the stores and equipment needed for the sledging program were at Hut Point and the dogs were taken back to Cape Evans. Mackintosh then divided his men into two parties, one with he, Spencer-Smith and Wild, and the second a six-man team under Joyce's command: of Joyce, Richards and Hayward as one unit and Cope, Gaze and Jack another. Stevens stayed at Cape Evans.

From now on Richards' life in the Antarctic is intimately involved with two men: the 40-year-old Ernest Joyce, an Antarctic veteran, and a Londoner with experience in snow conditions in Canada, Victor Hayward. They are a three-man sledging team and for the next six months they will share a tent, eat together, sleep together and live together. Together they will struggle to stay alive.

***

Over the months of October, November and December of 1915, the teams of men haul sledges laden with provisions from Hut Point, up the Great Ice Shelf and drop them at several depots across the first 70 or so miles of the Barrier, out to the Bluff Depot. They then return to Hut Point to bring out another load. The Bluff Depot is to be the principal base – that is the supply source – from which provisions are taken for the more southerly depots.

Sometimes the nine men travel together and at other times they travel as independent parties. On a good day, with a fully laden sledge, they make nine or ten miles. However, when the snow is very deep, they often cannot even move the laden sledge, so they have to relay and cover less miles a day. At other times they are travelling over sastrugi surface on the Barrier; ice which is as hard as marble with large hard parallel furrows usually running south-east and north-west. The furrows are sculptured by blizzards which regularly blow in these fixed directions. To Richards sastrugi looks like a frozen sea, and he finds hauling on this surface to be particularly wearisome.

In late October, Richards and Gaze persuade Joyce and Mackintosh to try out the dogs; to provide some extra assistance with the sledges. This change, to use the dogs on the Barrier, turns out to be decisive.

From then on, Con, Gunner, Oscar and Towser become an integral part of the men's lives. Richards is not sure why Joyce and Mackintosh were against using the dogs. They had used them before – but all their dogs had died – and this may have been a factor in Joyce being reluctant take the last few dogs onto the Barrier again. Mackintosh felt the dogs they had used were not a lot of assistance, with some refusing to pull even when their name was called out, so like Joyce he had little inclination to take dogs south. Mackintosh was also of the opinion that men and dogs were not compatible unless the men could ski. The pace of a man hauling a sledge with a heavy load in the snow was just trudge, trudge and trudge, with one foot a few inches in front of another. Dogs liked to go at a reasonable trot when they were pulling sledges and Mackintosh thought it would be quite impossible to marry the two. However, and surprisingly to Joyce, a man who had worked with dogs previously with Scott and Shackleton, the dogs quickly adapted to the men's slower walking pace.

Richards is delighted to have the dogs, especially as they are attached to the heavier laden sledge, he, Joyce and Hayward are pulling. Hayward quickly teaches him some of the basic commands necessary to control the dogs.

"It is easy to get them moving Rich. Simply yell 'Mush' or 'Hike' or 'Let's Go'."

"And to stop them I guess it is just 'Whoa'."

"Correct. Now to make them turn to the right you yell 'Gee'."

Richards is confused: "Gee, why 'Gee'?"

"Simple Rich. Gee you're right."

Richards shakes his head and smiles: "And to go left would be?"

"'Haw'. That will stump you as an Australian. Haw as in southpaw. A left hander."

Richards enjoys yelling instructions to the dogs, as do Joyce and Hayward, and they love having the dogs with them. They are harnessed to a sledge by rope in single file, not in a fan formation and at the front of them is the leading man, usually Joyce, who the dogs follow. Richards and Hayward are attached to the sledge separately, not in single file like the dogs.

Richards finds the four dogs to be as individual as humans and he quickly learns to recognize their every mood. Oscar, Gunner and Towser are Canadian Huskies, and they are lazy and quarrelsome, whereas Con is a Samoyed dog and completely different in character; he is the lead dog, good natured, lively and keen on hunting.

Richards has a favourite though and it is Oscar. He is a powerful brute, a massive dog at about 110lb with a broad leonine head and a forehead that Richards sees as being almost criminal like. Richards thinks he is disliked by the other dogs on account of his homosexual activities; he was named Oscar after Oscar Wilde.

The dogs are a welcome addition, and not simply for hauling – each dog can haul about 70 pounds – but for companionship and entertainment. Conversation in the evening often centres on some action by the dogs, such as how they jump up frightened when there is a sudden noise, like a heavy snow drop, or how they look longingly at the men, when the men are eating.

However, Joyce does not see them as being of long-term value. He says to Richards and Hayward: "We'll take them on south as long as they're fit, but we'll then sacrifice them."

Richards knows the story of Mawson's Antarctic adventure a few years previous: "Mertz, who was with Mawson, died after eating their dogs."

"Amundsen killed some of his dogs," says Hayward, "but only to feed the healthier dogs."

***

"You are the first Parson at 79 degrees south padre," says Wild to Spencer-Smith.

These two men, with Mackintosh, have dropped a load of stores 70 miles south from Hut Point, at the Bluff Depot position. They will now turn back to the north, to collect more provisions to bring to this location. Mackintosh wants a very large depot set up at the Bluff, and only after it is well stocked will stores will be taken further south for the other depots.

Mackintosh, Spencer-Smith and Wild enjoy each other's company, and Mackintosh and Wild have a lot in common. They are both navy men, the former having served as an officer on several ships with the merchant shipping company P&O and Wild had served with the Royal Navy on various vessels; battleships, cruisers and gunboats. In addition, they were both from Bedfordshire. Mackintosh was at

Bedfordshire Modern School for five years as a young boy and Wild lived at Eversholt, a tiny village in Bedfordshire, for ten years of his early life.

In their tent, the three of them have friendly debates on topics such as Home Rule, on how accurate is the sledge-meter, and on laymen taking scientific observations. They discuss a diverse range of topics; meals they would like to be eating, what could possibly happen with the war, politics of course and even religion seeing they have Spencer-Smith a padre in the tent.

Spencer-Smith revels in the discussions and often prompts Mackintosh and Wild to talk.

"Where were you born Skipper?" he asks Mackintosh one evening.

"India, Padre. But my mother left my father and took me and my brothers and sisters to Bedfordshire. I was told my father had Bright's disease. I wrote to him quite often, but sadly, I never did hear back from him."

"And you joined the navy?"

"Yes. At the age of 15, as an apprentice on a full-rigged sailing ship the *Cromdale,* and then on other ships, to become a Merchant Officer with the P and O Line."

"Tubby, what about you?" asks Spencer-Smith. "When did you join the navy?"

"Only ever been a navy man Smithy. Twenty years, non-stop since I was fifteen. I think I was five feet tall when I entered and have not grown more than three inches since."

"You are even shorter than Joyce," says Mackintosh.

"Got the name Tubby because of that, and I look heavy. But I was never going to be an officer like the Skipper here. I started as a Boy 2nd Class in HMS *Boscawen,* a Boys' Training Ship at Portland and made Petty Officer first class."

***

On some days in November and December Richards marvels at the weather. There are clear days where the sun is so hot that it scorches his skin and he must wear a large sun hat. However, the cold in the shade under the hat is so intense that his moustache and beard becomes frosted and covered with ice. His nostrils sting and tingle painfully. The weather is so bright and warm one afternoon that Hayward indulges in a snow wash, finding the snow to be a good substitute for water, soap and towel. When the weather conditions are mild, and it is relatively warm they travel in their singlets and 'drawers', which are underwear where the sides of the legs are open. A problem with warm weather at times is that the heat makes the snow surface like a piecrust, where the men break through the crust, sometimes up to their knees. The snow would take their weight for a second and then drop them down, usually only a few inches but occasionally a lot more.

At times they travel over a surface Joyce calls 'the Barrier Hush'. With a surface crust laying over softer snow the weight of the sledging party breaks the crust and the air from underneath it is expelled in a long 'hush-sh'. Richards finds the noise quite beguiling as it begins sharply and then slowly and eerily dies away in the distance.

The teams work non-stop during October, November and December, taking stores out from Hut Point onto the Barrier. However, in the last two months, Mackintosh's party, he, Spencer-Smith and Wild, stop returning to Hut Point, preferring to pick up supplies already deposited on the Barrier by the other teams. On one day, when they return to pick up more stores, Wild makes a pertinent diary note on his desire for seal meat.

"Couldn't find any fresh meat but had jam & onions extra."

Significantly, by mid-November, after having been in the field for only a short while, Spencer-Smith's feet and ankles are starting to give him trouble.

However, the six men of Joyce's team are still going back to Hut Point to pick up more stores, which gives them the opportunity to eat fresh seal meat. Seal meat is not taken on the sledges because it is too heavy. At Hut Point one evening Joyce cannot hide his delight in eating fresh meat: "Nothing better than having a good stock of seal meat, liver, kidneys and steak. What a bonzer meal."

When he is on the Barrier sledging, all Richards can hear is the crunch,

crunch of their fur clad feet in the snow, accompanied by the 'slee-e-e-e' of the sledge runners. At the five-minute rest spots, he crawls behind the sledge on the lee side, and pulls out from his shirt any little scraps he may have saved from the last meal; lumps of sugar, scraps of biscuits, crumbs of chocolate. They are dainty little scraps which can only be eaten with the tips of his fingers or he might lose them. When the rest is over, he stands, and finds he is stiff from head to heel. But he hobbles to his place in the traces, painfully puts on his harness, and after five minutes of hauling no trace of stiffness remains.

Richards finds he is always hungry, particularly when held up by a blizzard, because they then have to go onto reduced rations. He finds the hunger craving is worst when he is inactive. He also notices a funny pattern to his hunger pains, starting with a gnawing emptiness in his stomach so intense it dominates all thoughts to the point of obsession, a feeling close to panic. Then he feels he could eat anything, even his boots, but he learns to recognise this feeling and that it will pass eventually. His mind and body accepts somehow that he must go on without immediate nourishment. His hunger drowns all other troublesome feelings, such as burnt and blistered nostrils and lips, and chapped and blistered fingers. However, a pannikin of hot pemmican gives him immediate relief from his craving for food, as well as allowing him to more readily accept his other ailments.

***

The journey from Hut Point to the Bluff Depot location takes them across a heavily crevassed area but on most occasions the men simply gallop their sledges across the crevasses. This means they don't have to change course. Now and again one of the dogs would fall into a crevasse, or one of the men would, but they would be quickly jerked out.

At a five-minute spell, Richards and Hayward are standing next to each other, when Hayward suddenly disappears. Richards looks down and only Hayward's head and arms are visible.

Hayward yells: "Rich. Grab me! I must have been standing on a 'snow-lid' and punctured it."

Hayward had slipped through and saved himself by spreading out his arms. Richards goes to help but then he feels the earth slip from beneath him. He starts falling but manages to grab hold of the sledge and only goes down as far as his waist. Both crawl out and very gingerly step onto what they hope is sold ground, leaving two holes showing intensely blue against the surrounding white surface.

On one trip through the churned up crevassed area, Spencer-Smith, Mackintosh and Wild come up to an area where they can see a lot of crevasses ahead. Some are enormous, as wide as streets, and the three men know it would be a certain death if they attempt to cross them, so they work their way around. Then, Wild falls into one small crevasse but with one leg as it is only about a foot wide, although they see that it goes down a long way.

Then, just after Spencer-Smith calls out: "This is like playing a game hunt the crevasse," he falls completely into one.

He is dangling there, ten feet down the crevasse to the length of his harness, which is attached to the sledge. Wild is caught at the top of the edge, under the armpits and Mackintosh is lying across the crevasse gap with the sledge, somehow.

They manage to get Spencer-Smith out, by him bracing his body against the sides, using his knees and his back, and with Mackintosh and Wild pulling on a rope. The three of them then peer down the crevasse, but it is so deep they cannot see the bottom.

Spencer-Smith is shaken up: "It seemed a long time before I finished falling. I had this sensation of wondering when I'd stop descending."

Wild throws two or three big lumps of snow down but they disappear out of sight in the darkness.

"That was an unpleasant experience," says Spencer-Smith, "and it might have been serious if the sledge had been in a dangerous position, such as lying along the line of the crevasse. Laus Deo!"

He then holds up his hands. "My hands are gone, from holding onto the rope."

Wild smiles. He has a solution: "Stick them in your warming pan padre."

That night they talk over Spencer-Smith's lucky escape and compare his good luck with the misfortune on Mawson's expedition only four years before.

"You know about Mawson?" Mackintosh asks his two tent companions.

Wild shakes his head, but Spencer-Smith knows of Mawson's exploits. "I do Skipper. There were three men out on a sledging expedition, just like us. Then, one of the men plummeted down a crevasse, with one of their sledges and some of their dogs. Never heard from or seen again."

"And it gets worse Wild. Go on padre."

"Mawson and the other man had virtually no food to get back to base, so they ate their dogs. Then Mawson's companion died, so Mawson is then on his own."

"But he survives Wild," interrupts Mackintosh. "Due to his courage and his strong mind. He struggled on alone for about a month, eventually reaching his base."

"I doubt we will have anything like that to contend with," says Wild.

***

"Graft! Graft! Graft!" Spencer-Smith mutters to himself as he slogs his way along.

Unlike the others, he finds hauling to be extremely hard, and more so as his condition starts to deteriorate. By mid-November he is complaining to Mackintosh and Wild about the hauling being onerous, even after a long rest. His ankles are now sore all the time. By early December he is feeling rather seedy in the mornings, his tendons are getting worse and he has an extremely sore right foot. His afflictions are most unwelcome, with perhaps seven or eight hundred miles yet to be travelled.

He often talks to Wild about his health.

"My poor old neb and lips are very sore Tubby. I found it very heavy pulling today."

"It was a woolly surface," replies Wild.

"My right foot feels better though. I removed some dead flesh from the side of my big toe last night, and that seems to have done the trick."

As Spencer-Smith lies in his sleeping bag, to take his mind off his ailments he recites prayers in Latin, or thoughts of his friends at Cambridge trot in and out of his mind. He dreams and daydreams; such as one time where he had promised to preach in London, but had not written the sermon, nor could he remember where the church was.

He and Wild are sharing a tent with Mackintosh, whose actions at times Wild finds hard to fathom, but he does nothing to upset the harmony of the three-man team. He cannot understand Mackintosh's idiosyncratic ways. Mackintosh drops his mitts one morning and claims he cannot find them, but Wild manages to locate them. Then Mackintosh loses one of his finneskoe boots on a trip back to pick up stores, which Wild again finds for him. Then Mackintosh claims to have lost his watch but Wild sees it on the sledge. Mackintosh, somehow, breaks their compass. When his boot falls off the sledge he has Spencer-Smith go back a quarter of a mile for it. And he flummoxes Wild one day when he takes his boots and socks off at a lunch stop and runs around in the snow, claiming that it would be alright to go on the march without them.

But Wild simply accepts the situation in which he has been placed, plus he starts to devote more and more of his efforts to look after the ailing Spencer-Smith.

***

By mid-December, depots near the edge of the Barrier have been well-stocked, particularly the Minna Bluff Depot. Then, with fully laden sledges the nine men leave the Bluff Depot and head southward. They travel in the same two parties, one of Mackintosh, Spencer-Smith and Wild and the other of Joyce's team of six men and the dogs. They have about 280 miles to travel to Mount Hope.

They travel in two separate parties because Mackintosh prefers travelling in the night-time hours. He believes the colder night temperatures crisp the snow surface and this allows their skis and the sledges to glide a little more easily. Although it is not dark as the sun does not set in December. Whereas Joyce prefers travel in the daytime hours, as he does not like to upset the ordinary rhythm of he and his companions. Hence one party will often leap-frog ahead of the other, but they travel within a few miles of each other.

On Christmas Day of 1915, Mackintosh, Spencer-Smith and Wild enjoy the day together immensely, with a special meal of three supper rations of pemmican, plus two Bovril cubes and onions. They follow this with thick chocolate cocoa, biscuits, nut food and raisons. They sing 'While Shepherds watched' and 'Adeste Fideles', Wild gives a verse of 'Christmas Awake!' by himself and then Mackintosh hands out a cigar to both of them. Spencer-Smith cannot contain his pleasure: "This is the surprise of the century Skipper."

Wild is missing a drink, but a pipe of cigar tobacco makes his day.

"This is the best smoke I've had for years and years and this is the driest Christmas ever I've had, and I hope it will remain so."

On their Christmas Day, Richards, Joyce, Hayward, Cope, Gaze and Jack are camped only a few miles to the north of Mackintosh's tent. However, in sharp contrast to a Christmas Day of cigars, a sing-along, and a glut of food, Richards' and his companion's Christmas Day has no such luxuries. It is a day much like any other. That evening, after their standard fare of pemmican, supplemented with a little seal meat they had brought out from Hut Point, they discuss the practicalities of the day.

"How far have we come today Vic," asks Richards.

"Just under nine miles, eight and three quarters I think."

"What a Christmas Day," moans Joyce. "It was my fortieth birthday three days ago and here I am with nothing to smoke or drink."

"What do we have to drink for Christmas dinner?" laments Hayward. "A third of a mug of lemon juice. Anyway, here is a toast to absent friends."

"Yes," says Joyce. "I sometimes wonder how my old friends are, but I can't even drink to their health."

***

In early January 1916, because one of the three Primus stoves has developed a fault, three men in Joyce's six-man team have to be sent back. Joyce decides that Jack and Gaze must return, as they are not as strong as the others, and Cope is to go back with them. Both Jack and Gaze object strongly to being sent back, believing six men could all use the one primus. However, Joyce won't have this or anything else the two suggest, at any price. Gaze is not impressed with Joyce: "He's a rotter that man," he says to Jack and Cope. "I wouldn't trust him as far as I could kick him."

A few hours into their returning northbound travel, Gaze, Jack and Cope meet Mackintosh, Spencer-Smith and Wild. Gaze talks to Spencer-Smith – his cousin – to reveal his thoughts on Joyce: "He is out to play dirt on the Skipper AP. He intends to push on and try and meet Shackleton first, leaving the Skipper to do the hack work."

Gaze, Jack and Cope then continue northwards. They reach the *Discovery* hut and then Cape Evans without mishap. There, with Stevens, they wait for Mackintosh, Spencer-Smith, Wild, Joyce, Richards and Hayward to return.

Mackintosh's team were trailing Joyce's team by a few miles when Cope, Jack and Gaze turned back and at a lunch halt on the following day Richards looks back to the north.

"Look Joycey," as he points back along the route they have taken. "I can see Mack's party."

"It looks like they are overhauling us," says Hayward.

At 11 o'clock that night, the dogs start barking so Joyce goes outside, and to his surprise he finds Mackintosh's party camping next to their tent. They had been travelling non-stop since nine in the morning to catch up.

Joyce goes over to Wild: "You must have been working all hours Tubby."

"We had two lunches and marched eleven hours."

Wild goes on to explain: "The first ten miles were alright, fair wind and good surface, but after that the wind dropped and the surface got very bumpy. Still we caught you."

"You met Cope and the others returning?"

"Yes."

"I was pleased to see them leave," Joyce explains. "I had some words with both of them. Gaze, who was getting too big for his shoes, had to be taken down a peg. Jack is like an old gossiping washerwoman."

"It's the foreigners that do it," says Wild, who had little time for the two Australians, Gaze and Jack. "They give everybody a bad heart."

Richards remembers that they had seen a myriad of black objects spread over the white snow a week ago, and they had no idea what they were, until they came up to them and found the area littered with feathers. He asks Wild: "Tubby, did you kill a bird?"

"We did. It was a skua, and it was a most wonderful thing. It came flying over us and settled in the snow, so the Skipper and I got a large bamboo pole each and went for it. I caught it with a clout when it flew over my head, so we plucked, trussed and washed it before eating it."

Spencer-Smith adds: "It was about seven feet in the air when Tubby clubbed it. I think it had probably dropped from the blue on seeing us black specks below and came down hoping to find something to eat. Tubby cooked it."

"I boiled it for three hours and then fried it in pemmican fat and it was as tender as a chicken. We had a little dried onion with it, and six raison each for dessert. A wonderful meal."

Richards is envious, although Spencer-Smith did not enjoy the bird as much as Wild: "It was very fat and bilious but none the less nice. We topped off with rich cocoa and a few raisons."

In the morning Mackintosh tells Joyce to continue as before, so they travel as two separate teams, but close to each other. However, after a few hours Mackintosh suggests they tack the two sledges together, and travel as one team. Travelling in this new formation, with the six men pulling the two sledges now tied to each other, Joyce, Richards and Hayward immediately notice the lack of fitness of Mackintosh and Spencer-Smith.

In their tent that evening, Joyce says to Richards and Hayward: "It is clear to me, that Smith and the Skipper are obviously crooked."

"We do have the benefit of an extra heave on the occasions when the sledges are bogged though," says Richards.

"Yes, we are not delayed as much," replies Hayward.

Joyce is not convinced: "Those two are not pulling an ounce."

The six men – Joyce, Richards and Hayward, and Mackintosh, Spencer-Smith and Wild – and the four dogs, now work in unison, as a single detachment. Joyce is out front at the end of a long rope, as the leader, but he follows the directional guidance provided by Richards. Richards is navigating their route using a prismatic compass. Behind Joyce are Mackintosh, Spencer-Smith and Wild attached to the rope by harness, followed by the four dogs whose harness is also tied to the central rope. Behind the dogs, Richards is tied to one side of the sledges with an eight-foot rope, and Hayward similarly tied to the other side. 'Tied' is hardly the correct word, as knots cannot be loosened with the fingers in the cold conditions so all fastenings are made in such a way that they can be released by their hands encased in their fingerless mittens.

Richards is now the lone Australian, the only non-Englishman in the party of six men heading south to lay the final depots.

Sketch of Richards with his five English companions and four dogs.

CHAPTER 9

An ailing padre

"Excellent progress what?" says Hayward to Richards, after a day's pulling. They have reached the 80° S position, about 210 miles from Mount Hope. A depot of stores is put down and flags placed at specific distances and directions around the depot, so Shackleton can locate it more easily, and they too, on their return trip.

Over 10 miles were made that day, a similar distance covered on the few days before. The morning was overcast but the sun came out at about 11.30 which was the first they had seen it for some time. Most of them found it to be very hot and Joyce was travelling in his singlet with his drawers turned up.

They have been erecting smaller snow cairns between the depots, to help guide them on their return journey, in case the weather is poor. Every quarter or half an hour they stop and build a cairn of snow about four or five feet high.

"We need some black bunting," says Joyce as they start building up the first cairn past the 80°S depot.

Richards knows what Joyce is after. "I've an old pair of canvas trousers. They're covered with black blubber and soot. We can cut them up."

"Squares of about six inches will do."

"What's the bunting for Joyce?" asks Mackintosh.

"Cairn markers for our return journey Sir. They will be easier to spot with something dark on them."

They move on southwards, away from the 80°S depot with their next target being the location of the 81°S depot. Since the six men teamed up Richards has taken on the role of navigator. He takes a bearing on the known direction to Mount Hope and then he gives Joyce the leading man something in the distance to aim for. This could be a peak on the Trans-Antarctic Mountains that lie ahead on their path or at times simply on a cloud. In times of very poor visibility, when they have no feature in the distance ahead that they can see, Joyce and Richards steer using the 'black cairn method'. That is, they steer away from the piece of black cloth on a cairn behind, which can be seen. Richards takes a bearing of that cairn and works out the bearing they need to follow to stay on course to Mount Hope.

However, visibility is so poor on some days they cannot even see the cairn behind with the black bunting, so under these conditions Richards uses Joyce to steer by. Joyce is in the lead, at the end of a 20-30 feet long rope, and Richards is tied on to the bows of the sledge. He takes a bearing with the compass of the correct route and puts Joyce on that direction. After a short while they stop, Richards takes another bearing and readjusts Joyce's line if he has wandered. If there is no blizzard it is easy enough to steer on a cloud or some feature in the distance, or back steer from their own cairns.

Richards has been keeping a record in his diary of the bearing from one cairn to the next. He is not sure why he started doing this; it just seemed like a good idea, that the bearing might become useful.

***

Three men huddle around their Nansen cooker.

For 20 minutes Richards and Hayward stare at the hooch, as Joyce stirs it slowly, but they wait patiently as it always takes at least that amount of time to melt the snow and heat the pemmican. Joyce then adds in the last of their oatmeal which thickens the hooch a little, ladles it out carefully into three pannikins, and the men play their game of 'shut-eye' to select one each.

Rock-steady hands clasp the pannikin, as it is one of the worst things to happen, to drop their own hoosh. It is a catastrophe.

"Careful Vic," says Richards.

"You too Richie," he replies. "I dropped mine a week ago remember. What a calamity. It ranked with the fall of the British Empire. I scraped everything up off the floor cloth; a mix of pemmican, crumbs and finneskoe reindeer hairs. The heat of the meal was immediately lost, and the flavour never improved."

Joyce smiles: "You will never drop it again."

They finish their meal with a pannikin of tea with 20 lumps of sugar, and Hayward is satisfied.

"A feed for the Gods. I have the most comfortable feeling inside that I have known for some time. It is going to be very cold to-night. In fact even now I can hardly hold the pencil I am writing with and shall have to chuck it, till it gets warmer."

Richards has other things on his mind.

"The lack of fitness of Mack and Smithy is concerning me," he says.

Hayward nods. "I have noticed it too. I heard them talking to each other about being lame."

"To me they look exhausted," Richards replies. "Smithy complained to me a week ago that his knees were bad. He said he feels it very much in the ankles, and that his leg muscles are very sore."

Joyce is unsympathetic:" I don't think he or the Skipper has been doing much pulling."

Joyce shares his dislike for Macintosh with his two tent companions: "I never in my experience come across such an idiot to be in charge of men."

Despite these private comments by Joyce, Richards sees no outward antagonism between Joyce and Mackintosh; nothing hostile at all in their relationship. Joyce the ex-Petty Officer always respects the commissioned officer and he always addresses Mackintosh as 'Sir'. Joyce never loses the typical sailors old time respect for authority, and he always follows commands and loyally obeys Mackintosh's instructions.

***

The six men trudge on southward. The silence is acute, except for the crunch of feet in the snow and the faint swish of the sledge runners, and it is a profound silence, unless a blizzard is raging. Then their tiny party is lost in a howling shrieking wilderness of whirling snow.

There is little conversation on the trail as all their energies are needed for the job in hand. Richards rarely talks to anyone as he lumbers along, and the hours of a day's march seem endless, each step forward being a little in advance of the last. On some days he performs long useless computations of one sort or another in his head. It is not a deliberate act on his part but rather an automatic reaction to the monotony that is forced on him, a sedative or anodyne to the weariness of his body. At other times he looks at the peaks of the mountains on the Trans-Antarctic Mountain range, which are slowly coming closer. To amuse himself he sometimes guesses the bearing of a peak when they are starting the day, and then he guesses the bearing when they have finished for the day. He does it by eye, without the compass, and just purely for something to do, to try to work out in his own mind, the angle between the first two from the known distance they have travelled.

Richards tries to keep his mind occupied because there is such intense monotony trudging along one step a little in front of the other on the snowy surface. He has no idea what is going through his companions' minds or what they are thinking about. He believes they must be thinking of something, because there is not much to see. The Barrier is a featureless surface, although when it is clear they can look at and admire the mountains, but on many days, they are out of sight.

He often ponders on the simple things that make up his day's existence and he seldom thinks of the outside world. He has heard nothing from it since December 1914 and it is now late January of 1916. He has left all that behind and even the girl with the strawberry red lips on the train rarely crosses his mind. The only reality is what he and the other men see and do. However, he finds the pleasures of his day are just as satisfying as for someone in civilization. There is the shelter of the tent at the end of the day, the easing of a blizzard, a smooth-running snow surface, and ample food – at this stage of the journey. For Richards, these are the peaks above the drudgery of his day-to-day existence, and they give him a feeling of profound well-being.

At a rest break he talks to Spencer-Smith: "Smithy, what do you think about as you walk along?"

"I sometimes think of the dogs. Yesterday I saw that Con had a touch of sun blindness, so at the halts I heaped his head over with powered snow. He likes it and then he lies still with his head extended until we re-start."

Spencer-Smith goes on.

"Then today, with the cold headwind, I kept my Burberry helmet on all day, and I dreamt through what was the longest afternoon of the trip for me, so far. I was thinking of a sermon; they shall mount up with wings, and more, which is the last verse of Isaiah 11, and then I recounted a poem, Life and Death."

Richards looks at Hayward.

"And you Vic, what do you think about?"

"Nothing. It's all just a terrible silence and monotony Richie. All I do is think and think and think and only think and pull and pull and pull and only pull. I just don't have enough breath to converse and I don't want to.

All I want to think about are things which will take me out of these surroundings to other and more homely and pleasing ones."

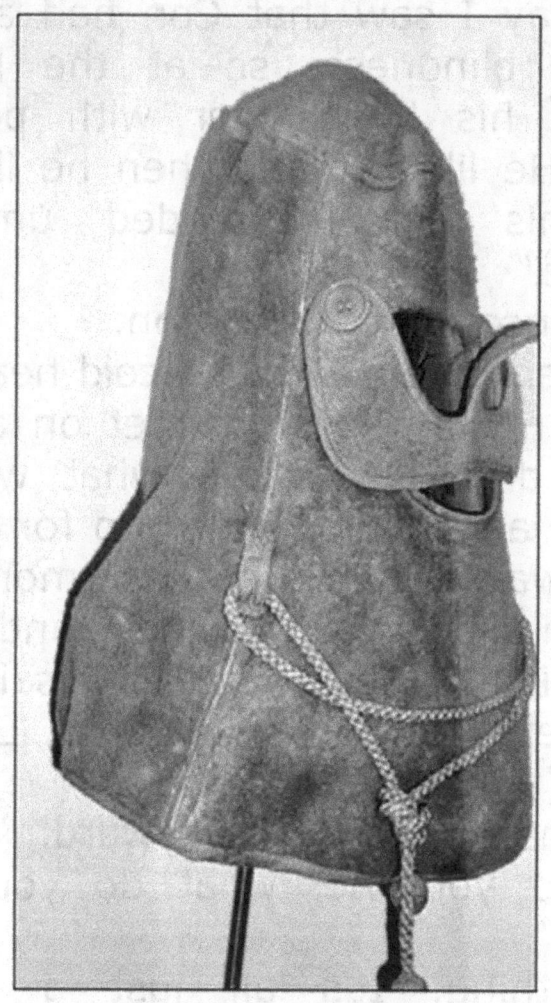

Burberry helmet.

***

"You know why the sledge-meter stopped today?" Richards asks Hayward and Joyce one evening. They have no idea why.

Richards smiles: "Dog turds. Stuck to the wheel."

The three of them laugh, and then Richards has another question. "You were not sure the dogs would last Joycey, were you?"

"No. I thought that if they were still fit by now, we would take them on south a little more and then sacrifice them."

Richards, as well as Joyce, is now fully aware that the wellbeing of the dogs is paramount. He starts to watch over them with a zealous care because he realises that just one bite on a foot might mean a significant loss to the whole party. They cannot afford to lose even one dog as that would be a loss of a quarter of the dog's pulling power, even though the dogs don't pull as much as a man.

"They are in splendid form Richie, give them a hot hoosh at least twice a week, it's worth it for all the wonderful work they are doing. If we can keep them going, I guarantee they'll live in comfort the remainder of their days."

Richards knows they must be looked after very carefully: "I'm almost certain we shall have Smithy or Mack on the sledge one day."

It is not only the dogs that need special care, as the primus cooker used by Mackintosh, Spencer-Smith and Wild has suddenly broken down. Richards tries to fix it, but without any success at first because he hears Wild yell to him from the other tent: "still working rotten". However, Richards works on the cooker on the next day with some success as he is delighted to then hear Wild's loud voice: "Primus working Richie. All bands now."

***

They put down food and fuel at 81°S, and then push on to cover another 70 miles to the next point of latitude, 82°S. By mid-January Richards and his five companions reach that point, 82°S, and they are now within 100 miles of Mount Hope. Once again provisions are left for Shackleton's party and themselves; enough to make the trek back to the 81°S depot on their homeward run.

After setting up the 82°S depot, Joyce and Richards speak to Mackintosh. They know Mackintosh's original plan was for Joyce, Richards and Hayward to go back from here.

"Sir," explains Joyce, "there are two problems with sending us back. First of all, one of the cookers is showing faults now and again so it would be folly to split us up. And secondly, Rich and I are very worried about the health of the padre, and you as well Sir."

Richards supports Joyce. "We think it would be suicide if you, Smithy and Tubby went on alone."

Mackintosh acquiesces to Joyce and Richards' request for their team to continue. Richards thinks Mackintosh has finally realised that it is the interests of all six men that the entire sledging party should stay together. Or that he may have sensed some sort of mutiny if he had tried to send them back.

Before continuing south from the 82°S depot Mackintosh makes Richards sign an agreement, which Mackintosh dictates and Spencer-Smith writes out two copies on pages of foolscap. It is a replica of an Agreement that Richards had already signed, when being interviewed by Mackintosh in Sydney. Once again it spelt out that Richards had 'to obey the lawful commands of the above-named Sir Ernest Shackleton CVO or those appointed by him' and to 'hold secret all work in connection with the Expedition', as regards publishing on return to civilisation. Mackintosh and Richards sign both copies.

When Hayward asks Richards why he had to sign a new Agreement, Richards says: "My guess it that it suddenly occurred to him that this bugger Richards may blow the gaff when I get back. I had better seal him up."

Hayward smiles: "And I guess that no other legal agreement has been made closer to the South Pole, or the North Pole."

The six men and four dogs push on southward from the 82°S depot. They are still travelling well, averaging almost 13 miles a day, because they have a lighter load to haul after stocking up the depots. The Trans-Antarctic Mountain range is slowly becoming closer, and closer.

Over these days Spencer-Smith's condition worsens, and he clearly has symptoms of scurvy, but he struggles on. He makes occasional diary notes on what is going through his mind as he wills himself along but there are no notes of wanting to stop, or give in. In his mind he simply has to keep going.

***

At the end of a day's hauling Wild unpacks the sledge with Richards and Hayward. With help from Mackintosh and Richards he then erects his tent, lays down the ground cloth and helps a limping Spencer-Smith inside. Wild then cooks the dinner hoosh for Mackintosh, Spencer-Smith and himself. One evening, after making sure Spencer-Smith is comfortable, he goes across to the tent of Joyce, Richards and Hayward.

"Tubby, how is Smithy?" asks Richards.

"He sometimes tells us how he's feeling, usually when he wakes each morning. He often tells of his dreams; one where he dreamt that the war was over. He sometimes feels seedy, and for some time now he's been talking about his sore tendons."

Richards is impressed with Spencer-Smith's resolution: "I admire his efforts. He's ahead of me on the rope and I can see him limping. He's obviously in pain."

"But he isn't improving," says Wild. "Yesterday he said his legs were very stiff and it was quite painful walking, and at lunch he said he nearly fainted. We gave him an extra Bovril cube, but he thinks his heart is rather ricked."

"Both the Skipper and Smith are obviously crooked," says Hayward. "I am behind the Skipper and he is not pulling an ounce. He appears to have a sprained knee and is painful to watch."

Wild knows just how poorly Spencer-Smith is: "The padre's knees are also very bad. They're swollen and with what looks like a great bruise above and below the knees, especially the right."

Joyce is unimpressed. "No wonder he's walking along like an old man. I think the Skipper and he ought to have gone back with the other party, but now they are with us they will have to leg it out or camp until we come back. Time is too precious to waste, and I expect it will mean carting them on the sledge."

The condition of Spencer-Smith and Mackintosh concerns the others, but there is little that can be done – except to go on – because in their minds, the depots for Shackleton have to be placed.

It is now near the end of January – they had left the Cape Evans hut at the start of September – and the six men are over 300 miles south of the huts. Joyce is now preoccupied in determining which mountain in the range ahead is Mount Hope. Richards, along with Joyce, Hayward and Wild are reasonably fit but Mackintosh and Spencer-Smith are faltering and provide little help with the sledge pulling. Then, just 30 miles from Mount Hope, Spencer-Smith's failing health impinges dramatically on the dynamics of the six-man party.

CHAPTER 10

Facing the 360-mile return trek

"Skipper, depot me here and carry on to Mt. Hope without me," calls out Spencer-Smith.

"Joyce. Stop," yells Mackintosh.

Hayward bawls at the dogs: "Whoa," and they stop pulling.

Spencer-Smith sits down in the snow.

"I can't go any further. It's just too difficult to walk. We have done about two hours this morning, but it has been a struggle. My knees above and below are getting heavier, hotter and more painful every step."

The five men stand around Spencer-Smith and Joyce leads the conversation.

"Well, what do we do?" he says.

Richards is the first to respond: "We can't go on with Smithy."

"And there's no point in turning back now," says Mackintosh. "We have to place the depot for Sir Ernest at Mount Hope, and we are only a few days away."

Spencer-Smith then offers the only practical solution: "Put up a tent for me and pick me up on the way back. I'm happy to stay. I'll be quite alright."

"We have no other choice," says Hayward.

"Sir, why don't you stay with Smithy?" suggests Joyce.

Richards agrees. "That sounds like a good idea Mack. You seem to be limping too."

"A rest might do you good Skipper, make you more fit for our long journey back," adds Hayward.

" No. It is my duty, as leader of the party, to see the last depot is made."

"Let's pitch one of the tents," says Joyce.

They put up the conical tent and leave Spencer-Smith there, in his sleeping bag, with a supply of calico bags containing cocoa, oatmeal, cheese, sugar and pemmican, and a primus next to his bag. He is perfectly cheerful and confident that after the rest he will be able to make the return journey.

Wild reassures him: "By the time we get back you will be on your feet again."

"I expect us to be back again under the week," says Joyce.

"Eheu! But it's no use howling," are Spencer-Smith's final words before the others leave.

Spencer-Smith is alone, but he is not perturbed as he anticipates the others will be back within a few days. They have left him a bottle of lime juice in case his complaint is some form of scurvy, which he doubts. He is comfortable and is sure he will be all right – except for loneliness and disappointment – which he thinks is probably merited.

***

"Let's pray this blizzard clears soon," says Mackintosh.

"Do many blizzards last more than a day or two?" asks Richards.

Joyce smiles ruefully. "They can last a week Richie. I'm hoping Provi will look on us and give us a June day tomorrow."

Richards decides to go outside to relive himself, but the blizzard is stronger than any he has experienced so far. As soon as he steps outside the tent snow drives into his face, forming a sheet of ice over his eyes. He also finds it impossible to stand. So, he drops to his hands and knees and crawls away from the tent. After doing his toilet he tries to regain the tent, but it is not easy. The tent is only a few yards away, but Richards cannot see it. His only guide is the direction of the wind.

The five men are camped; in the one tent. Spurred on by their anxiety to place the last depot, and to get back to Spencer-Smith, they made good headway, but a blizzard has stopped their progress. They have a light load on because they only need to carry provisions for the last depot for Shackleton and their own use; and the dogs are pulling strongly.

Joyce is not unhappy with the short delay: "A rest will do us all good, dogs and us."

Circumstances have put five men together in one tent for the first time, but there is a feeling of camaraderie, and even Joyce sees their cramped conditions in the tent as pretty fair. On the first night Mackintosh, Wild, Joyce and Hayward play 'auction bridge' – a variation on the normal game of bridge – with Richards an interested onlooker. Joyce and Hayward are the winners.

After two days the blizzard clears, and they move on. They are now quite close to the mountains and are steering directly for a detached rounded mountain a few thousand feet high which Joyce is confident is Mount Hope. They come onto a crevassed area and are forced to camp.

That night Wild tells everyone: "It's just twelve months today since we left the ship. The longest time I've been off a ship for over twenty years."

In the morning they find a passage through a maze of crevasses; thousands of tons of ice churned up to a depth of about 300 feet. They are all roped together and fatalistically believe they will have no trouble; which fortunately they don't, and then they reach the Beardmore Glacier.

"Have you ever seen a scene so full of colour?" asks Richards, as he and the others stare at the twenty-five miles wide glacier stretching away to the south. The blue ice of the glacier has a broad ridge in its middle, of a brownish colour, and the glacier is flanked by sheer steep rock faces, where the exposed rock is very black.

"A most wonderful sight," says Joyce.

"Look," Richards suddenly calls out as he points at a dark patch on the glacier. "Is that a tent? Is it Shackleton's tent? Vic, pass me the glasses."

Wild watches on eagerly because if it is Shackleton, his brother Frank will be with him. Richards lies down and peers through the binoculars at the shape, which appears to be just like a tent, and he wonders if anyone will come out of it. But there is no sign of life, the dark shape is a rock.

Their final task is completed when they lay the final depot, and at camp that night, they discuss the day.

Joyce is happy: "I'm very pleased to see our work done at last. We've left

The Boss two weeks provisions and two full tins of oil. They ought to be alright."

"And they can't miss it," says Hayward. "Lashed to that old broken sledge of Scott, and with the large flag on top."

"I'm at peace," says Mackintosh. "We have placed all the depots for Sir Ernest."

"How are you Sir?" Wild asks.

"Quite lame Wild."

"Let's look at your legs," says Joyce. He sees a considerable area of blue discoloration behind Mackintosh's knees and knows the problem: "I think it may be scurvy Sir."

After sipping from his pannikin of cocoa, Wild makes another of his engaging announcements to everyone: "You know, cocoa will never taste this good when we get back."

Richards does not sleep that night. He is pleased they have finished their task, to lay the final depot, but he is worried about Spencer-Smith. He tosses and turns in his bag, thinking of his companion miles away on his own, and cracks like pistol shots from movement of the Beardmore Glacier keep him awake all night long.

***

"Homeward bound Tubby, 360 miles to go," says Joyce to Wild the next morning. "I think with the help of good old Provi we ought to be at Hut Point in a month."

On Shackleton's *Nimrod* expedition of 1909, Shackleton, Marshall, Adams and (Frank) Wild were returning from a southbound journey and they took 36 days to travel from the foot of the Beardmore Glacier to the hut.

Wild is very pleased: "Thank God we are on the back trail. They say enough is as good as a feast well I've had my feast of sledging this season. Now for a good run back where I hope to find some bacco."

It is late January of 1916 when Mackintosh, Joyce, Richards, Wild and Hayward leave Mount Hope. They pick up their outward trail and travel well, with the dogs, Oscar, Con, Towser and Gunner, pulling energetically as they are now heading north. At camp that evening the five men huddle around the

Primus stove and they are optimistic, as well as very pleased with themselves.

"We should pick up Smithy tomorrow around eleven," says Joyce.

Wild is typically down-to-earth: "In all probability he'll have to be put in the sledge."

Whereas Richards is very concerned: "I'm worried about him. You know, he blamed his problems on a tear in his clothing not scurvy or his health."

"Well," says Hayward, "if you get a tear in your windproof clothing you can get a sort of a frost bite in a blow through that tear. I've seen flesh, which is red through a tear, because of the wind that comes in there. That's what he thought had happened."

"I feel for him," Richards says. "A sick man, with no one closer than 300 miles away to the north, and us to the south. He has no idea when we'll return."

Richards goes on: "I'm worried we may not even find him, and it might be very difficult if the weather is poor. We have to locate a little conical shaped tent in a wilderness of ice and snow where there are no features, and nothing to guide us."

Joyce moans.

"How are your eyes Joyce?" asks Mackintosh.

"Nasty attack of snow blindness today Sir, like they're full of coal dust from a steam train. That's why I went off the lead position and turned the steering over to you. Had to bind up my eyes with a piece of cloth and join everyone at the sledge."

"We could see you falling and stumbling about, because of the uneven surface," says Hayward.

Joyce smiles: "I was falling down like a jumping jenny."

Wild drops a sliver of cocaine into a pannikin, waits for it to dissolve, holds Joyce's head back, opens an eyelid and then dribbles a few drops of the liquid into Joyce's eye. Joyce cries out in pain.

Wild smiles. "Just like the night last year heading back to Hut Point, when we heard the Skipper groaning eh Joycey. Remember? He was in agony with a toothache."

"I was in positive agony," says Mackintosh.

Joyce tells Richards and Hayward what happened.

"In the medical case there was nothing to ease him. I could only think of methylated spirits, so I gave him the bottle, together with some cotton wool. He placed the cotton wool with spirit on the tooth, a second elapsed and then a yell, the sound of which must have penetrated to Cape Evans."

Richards and Hayward start laughing, but Mackintosh interrupts: "The toothache was cured, but the inside of my mouth was raw."

Joyce explains: "The temp of the spirit was the same temperature as the air, 82 degrees of frost. It had the same effect as boiling liquid."

"The skin had peeled off the inside of my mouth, exposing a raw sore, as the result of the methylated spirit. My tooth was better though."

"You should have seen yourselves when you arrived at the *Discovery* hut," says Hayward. "Skipper you looked dazed, Tubby had an ear completely frost bitten as well as his nose and one foot and Joycey, your hands and nose and feet were gone. You all looked awful."

Wild lightly dismisses his ailments with nautical terms: "My port lug and starboard toe were slightly frost-bitten, that's all."

Richards is taken back when Joyce mentions that Wild's big toe had to be amputated and part of his ear had to be cut off as well. Hayward gives Richards a few details of the operation on Wild. It was while they were at the *Discovery* hut at Hut Point waiting for the sea ice to free properly so they could walk to Cape Evans.

"Conditions were far from sanitary with blubber soot and grease everywhere, but lucky we had Cope with us, who worked under extreme difficulties. He told us that he was a botanist and his only surgery of any sort was when he cut up a dead dog. Tubby's toe was the colour of soot and almost horribly gangrenous. His ear was dripping vicus matter continuously. It was tough watching Tubby stick the pain."

Wild had not mentioned the loss of his toe or the top of his ear to Richards or anyone else, nor had he even thought to even make a note of the amputations in his diary. Slightly perturbed by people discussing his problems, he takes the discussion away from his old ailments. "We did find a leg of mutton there though."

"A lucky discovery that was," says Joyce. "It had been there since Scott's first expedition, so it was nearly 15 years old, but it was still fresh."

"And fresh meat is always acceptable what!" says Hayward. "We enjoyed the mutton immensely."

Mackintosh, Joyce and Wild then relate more of the hardships they experienced sledging in March of the previous year. They tell Richards and Hayward about fastening and unfastening buttons or ropes, where they have to remove their mitts. Their fingers would 'go'. They explained that in a wind with snow drift, even at minus 20 degrees Fahrenheit, they could not expose their hands for more than a minute or two, without getting the fingertips frozen. If their gloves were warm, they found their fingers usually recovered quickly and there would be no side effects, except a little tenderness which lasted for a few days. However, if the fingers took longer than a few minutes to recover they would blister and be very sore for a week or more, after which all the skin would peel off. They found that if frostbite reached below the skin of the hand or foot the result was a water blister, like in a bad burn. What worried them the most was if the frost bite became deep-seated, then the blood vessels would not recover and it could lead to gangrene, as it had with Wild's toe and part of his ear.

"That's what it is going to be like in a few weeks," says Mackintosh. "Let's hope we are safely back at the huts by then."

Wild remembers another incident from the previous year.

"We did get a laugh one night," he says. "We had started with great hopes that morning but found we couldn't move the sledge. So, we took the double runners off and made another attempt, then Joyce suddenly goes off."

Joyce grins. "It was easy pulling and I called back 'by Gollams, this is better already', but I had forgotten to hitch on my harness."

Wild smiles as he remembers: "By the way we didn't see the humour of this till night-time, and then we laughed until we cried talking about it."

"I swear this place, once I return home, will never see me again," says Mackintosh.

***

The sounds of dogs scrapping and men calling grew fainter, and fainter and then Spencer-Smith could hear nothing. His world had become silent, but he was not overly concerned, even looking forward to a few days' rest, anticipating he would recover while the others were away.

He lies in his sleeping bag, where he reads, and he dreams. In one dream he and the others meet Shackleton and Frank Wild, with Frank wearing a gold laced hat and Shackleton is clean shaven. At another time, half-asleep and half-awake he plans a comedy which he names as "Brown, Jones and

Robinson". He finds the dialogue rattles off beautifully until he begins to think of writing it down.

After three days he imagines the others have now laid the final depot and that they should reappear on the next day. However, he is concerned because his knees feel no better and they will find him unwell. He twice goes outside to try to enjoy the sunshine, but his knees become painful immediately, and he also feels a little funny in his chest so he thinks his heart might be a little feeble.

Spencer-Smith lives in a complete silence, apart from the noise of the wind and occasional sounds from movements of the snow and ice refreezing and splitting due to changes in temperature. His sleeping bag, two mats and a floorcloth under him become sopping wet.

By the sixth day on his own, he makes calculations on the distance the others had to travel to Mount Hope, surmising that their delayed absence could be accounted for. He makes a note in his diary that he feels 'very rotten', and there is no sign of the others at 5.p.m. on that day.

However, on the next morning he hears dogs barking and men's voices. They are such strange sounds after days of almost complete silence, and they cheer him immediately.

He calls out cheerfully: "Laus Deo!"

Mackintosh, Joyce, Wild, Hayward and Richards find Spencer-Smith still in his sleeping bag.

"We felt for you Smithy," says Richards. "A small speck on this ice shelf after we disappeared to the south a week before. You must have been very lonely indeed."

"I'm very glad to see you. It has been a trying time."

"How are you feeling padre?" asks Mackintosh.

"Horribly Skipper. I can't walk. I have terrible pains in the back of my knees, which I think it is from tears in my windproof trousers. My legs are black and swelled up."

"It may be scurvy," says Joyce, "but I don't think so. Your gums and eyes don't show it."

Wild is keen to start moving: "There is only one thing to do Smithy. We have to put you on the sledge."

Richards realises the implications. The extra weight will pull down their speed and it is being optimistic to think they will now be able to do more than 10 or 12 miles a day. He has concerns, but the others have few doubts that they will be back safely at the hut by early March.

Wild is philosophical: "I'm afraid that will make us rather longer getting back. Still it can't be helped."

It is early February and all the depots have all been put in place. The six men are back together and heading north, with about 330 miles to reach the *Discovery* hut at Hut Point. There are depot points every 70 miles where they can pick up a week's provisions to take them onto the next depot, but Spencer-Smith is unable to walk and has to be carried on the sledge.

From this day on, Spencer-Smith lives in his sleeping bag. He is carried from the sledge to the tent in it at each lunch stop and at the end of every day.

CHAPTER 11

The blizzard

"Our only place is the bag, "Richards realises.

"No meal till noon. Half rations just in case the blizzard lasts for more than a day."

The experienced Joyce has made the decision to reduce the food intake for him, Richards and Hayward. A blizzard has hit them, within a day after setting off with Spencer-Smith, so the six men wait in their two tents. In his tent Mackintosh looks at his two companions – Spencer-Smith and Wild – and then talks, almost to himself.

"What a weird scene this is. Here lie three forms stretched out, one with a hand holding a book and the other only with a portion of his face appearing out of the bag."

Wild and Spencer-Smith say nothing.

"And around our feet lie the cooker, various bags, finneskoe, all this enclosed in a small green tent. What queer places and positions man will place himself."

Wild is thinking of the more practical aspects: "It's now our fifth month of sledging Sir, and I hope another month will finish it."

But even with thoughts of only a month to finish, Mackintosh is despondent.

"One month of the nightmare of putting on the finneskoe. You know Wild, for me, getting away in the mornings is the bitterest time. My finneskoe are always frozen stiff, and I struggle to force my feet into them. I call it my hour of discontent, as it always takes me anything from a quarter to half an hour of hard struggle and pain for each foot. Especially if one happens to have a chapped heel, which I have."

Wild has no sympathy for Mackintosh: "Sir, I'm not cold but I am wet through. But I can't shift clothes. I haven't got any."

"Wild, in times like this I am encouraged by words of Emerson, a poet you may not have heard of. Listen to this; it is from a book I have here called 'Being and Doing'.

> So nigh is grandeur to our dust,
> So near is God to man,
> When duty whispers well I must,
> The Youth replies 'I can!'"

Mackintosh stops talking and suddenly calls out: "Heads under".

Wild and Spencer-Smith put their heads under their sleeping bags. Mackintosh stands up and lifts the corner of the tent's groundsheet. He digs a square out of the snow with a knife, lifts it out, and after finishing his toilet he puts the square of snow back again.

This blizzard only lasts one day.

***

"We seem to be making rather fantastic distances Vic," Richards says to Hayward one evening a few days later.

Like Richards, Hayward's thoughts are dominated by how far they still have to travel to reach the *Discovery* hut. So in early February he starts keeping a simple table in his diary of the date, the distance travelled for the day and the number of miles left to reach Hut Point.

They are travelling well, in a slightly different formation than before, as Spencer-Smith is on the sledge. Joyce is usually in the lead on a long rope, and he is followed by the leading dog Con and then Gunner who are in a single file behind Joyce. Then follows Towser with Wild one side of him and Mackintosh the other, and then Oscar the last dog is closest to the sledges, flanked by Richards and Hayward.

Hayward is also happy with their progress: "Yes Rich. We are, considering the load with Smithy strapped on top, and there are often just four of us pulling, and the four dogs. Mack can do no more than walk along most of the time."

There is often a southerly wind and the dogs are eager, so they manage to cover 17 and 18 miles a day at first. They reach the at 82° S depot about 280 miles out from Hut Point, where they pick up a week's rations to take them on to the next depot. The good weather continues, and they arrive at the 81° S depot – 210 miles out from Hut Point – within another seven days.

The tent conversation of Joyce, Richards and Hayward often turns to the health of Mackintosh, as well as Spencer-Smith. Richards feels for Wild.

"Poor old Tubby has to lift Smithy and carry him off the sledge, and then back onto it each morning. I noticed his bag is wet through. He lives in it all the time."

"There's no way of drying it," says Joyce.

Richards is the nearest to Spencer-Smith when they are travelling and elaborates on what he sees and hears.

"On the sledge he lies down inside his bag and I cannot see him, although I'm close to him on the bow of the sledge. He has the bag flap right over his face and part of the time he seems unconscious. At times I hear him uttering wandering thoughts and at other times I hear him reciting a prayer in Latin."

Even Joyce, the more hard-edged man of the three, starts to feel for Spencer-Smith: "Poor chap but he's a

Briton. No complaint from him. We shall have to put our right foot forward as I'm rather afraid we shan't get him in on time. Still, no one can do any more than we are."

"The Skipper is now very lame," says Hayward.

Joyce looks closely at Hayward: "I can see that your gums are black Vic and protruding too."

"I know. And I'm slightly black at the back of the knees."

Richards then lets on that he had been looking at his teeth that morning: "I have a little pocket glass mirror. I felt my gums were swelling and I wanted to look at them and I noticed sort of black blisters here and there on them. Joycey, have a look."

Joyce squints into Richards mouth, and sees the blisters.

"Scurvy Richie. I think the scurvy has got us all and there's only one thing for it, fresh meat."

Wild crawls into their tent.

"I need some of the emergency ration of Bovril, for the padre, and I had to get out for a minute."

"What's the matter Tubby?" asks Richards.

"It's the Skipper. He's still as selfish as ever. He lets Smithy lay on a boot while he has two big fur mitts for pillows."

Joyce repeats his irritation with Mackintosh: "I was watching the old man today and he is very bad. He's pulling about the same number one rat power. Still, we ought to be in within three more weeks."

***

The five men plod on, each man lost in his own thoughts. On clear days Richards is overawed by the Trans-Antarctic Mountain Range they are travelling close to and because of his interest in minerals he spends his time often contemplating the land and the possible minerals of the area. He, Joyce and Wild discuss this topic and as a result the three of them – optimistically – think it might be a good idea to make a trip back into this area of the mountains in the following summer. They discuss undertaking a detailed examination of the rocks, as of course it had never been done.

Spencer-Smith's thoughts are often on his weakening condition. His gums are very sore, so he keeps taking lime juice, but he feels his health fluctuates wildly. His gums seem to improve but on the next day they might be feeling poorly. He also thinks about people from home. On one day he spends most of the day in thoughts with two of his old 'Edinburgh pals', on the following day's afternoon he keeps imagining 'tired man's' jobs for himself, and on another day his mind keeps wandering back to a pleasant afternoon he once spent in South Square, Gray's Inn.

They manage to travel from the 81° S depot to the 80° S depot in another seven days, but Richards starts to notice that every activity, everything they do, is taking a little longer. Joyce, with his years of naval discipline has been religiously waking at 5.30am and calling to everyone to turn out, but occasionally Joyce now sleeps in, and they start their day an hour or more later than usual. From Joyce's call to turn out, to when they are on the move is now taking more than the two hours it took a week ago. Lassitude and weakness have hit all of them, as they slowly and wearily clamber out of their bags, have their morning hoosh, roll up their bags, strike the tent and stow the sledges.

If it is snowing when they wake, they often make the easy decision to defer starting because it is 'too thick' to get underway, rather than driving themselves to start. Then, on the march, on days where heavy snow is falling creating a bad light for steering, there are many stoppages where they search ahead for the cairns they had laid on the outward journey.

It is February 11 when they reach the 80° S depot and restock up with provisions. It is a wonderfully clear day; which Joyce finds remarkable at that latitude.

"A strange day," he says to Richards and Hayward that evening. "That blue sky is very unusual. We call this the gloomy stretch, as no party has experienced good weather in this latitude. Not Scott or Shacks."

They are now only 140 miles from the hut.

***

On February 12 they set off for the next depot – the Bluff Depot – about 70 miles away, but their progress is now being hindered by their lethargy; from the scurvy which is taking a stronger hold on all of them.

Sledge-meter.

Then their sledge-meter breaks, but Hayward keeps making a note – now a calculated guess – on how many miles they make daily, and the probable number of miles to safety; the *Discovery* hut at Hut Point. Richards starts showing more and more of an interest in their progress.

On February 15 he asks Hayward: "How far now Vic?"

"Not a lot more than a hundred miles, I think."

"But we seem to be making less each day."

Hayward looks at his diary.

"We are. For the first few days after leaving the 80-degree depot we travelled reasonably well, making an estimated 10 or 12 miles a day, but today I estimate we only made eight miles. It could have been the surface as it was pretty fair in the forenoon, but in the afternoon it was the most rotten surface we have experienced since we have been out."

In his tent Mackintosh thinks of home, as February 15 is the anniversary of his wedding day. His thoughts turn back to his wedding of five years ago. What a change in his life he says to himself. Spencer-Smith hears him talking.

"Are you okay Skipper?" he asks.

"Yes padre. I am just asking myself what I am doing here. And such a thought makes me wish I was back at home with my dear ones who are waiting so patiently."

***

As their weakness increases, they gradually jettison everything they can to lighten their load. They leave their second sledge behind, then the broken sledge-meter, and other items like extra shovels and ice-picks are tossed aside.

With winter approaching, conditions outside and inside the tent start to become diabolical, making life even more miserable. They all have a thick growth of beard which is a great hindrance in low temperatures as their breath freezes onto their whiskers. The beard grows, until they have about a pound weight to carry, to say nothing of the coldness of the ice against their faces. At the end of each day's hauling they have severe frostbites on their faces and their necks and cheeks are often quite stiff and swollen, making it painful to turn around or laugh. Hayward realises his mistake and that he should not be surprised as even in the coldest winds he still marches without a hat on.

In their sleeping bags their clothes are only damp, but when they get out of the bag, they freeze hard. Plus, when they must get out of the bag for their hoosh, they find on their return a stiff hard board instead of a soft damp sleeping bag.

Richard struggles to sleep, every night. He places the iced-up hard lid of his iced-up sleeping bag over his head, but at first nothing occurs. Then, after a little time, lumps of ice fall on his face as his breath thaws the ice off. He pushes pieces of ice to one side or sometimes he just lets it thaw into water and absorb into his clothes. He, like the others, just lies there, twisting and turning. Towards morning as the temperature drops, he finds the top of his bag frozen again. He then hears one of the others groaning and cussing as they try to bring back a frozen part of their body. Invariably it is not long before he is cussing and groaning, for the same reason.

The 'fun' of sledging has gone completely for Hayward now, and he becomes depressed, thinking of his Ethel more and more. He has drawn a picture of her in his diary and on one evening he has an extra-long and lingering look at this picture. On the next morning he wakes feeling quite homesick and rotten, more so than he has felt for months. He then decides to refrain from looking at her picture again for some time, so he does not experience the same morbid feelings.

At every camp and at every midday halt Wild continues to lift Spencer-Smith – in his sleeping bag – from the sledge to the tent. Mackintosh his tent mate is now almost an invalid so practically the entire care of Spencer-Smith falls on Wild's shoulders. He is the only other occupant of that tent. Richards is astounded at the personal care and reverence that Wild shows tending to Spencer-Smith, on every single day. The young man has never seen such devotion by one human towards another.

"What is that saying?" he says to Hayward and Joyce one night. "There are some things that have great value but no glitter and that is Tubby to me. He is so patient, so long-suffering the way he looks after Smithy, but he is always good-humoured."

When Spencer-Smith is awake he does not gripe or grumble. He does not complain, is often ready with a cheery word and he does his best to make the others' task as easy as possible. Lying on the sledge, he now dreams or thinks of England every day. His thoughts wander around on different topics as he slips in and out of consciousness. At times the sledge tips over completely as it veers wildly across the hard-parallel furrows of sastrugi surface, but thankfully without injuring him or causing any serious damage to the sledge. On one day, he is overjoyed when his favourite dog Gunner comes to visit him. The dog had managed to get out of his harness while the others were putting up the tent.

Joyce, Richards and Hayward find they have less and less to say to each other in the evenings, because they are so tired and worn out.

"The surface on this stretch is like ploughing ones way through treacle on stilts," is Joyce's only comment as he stirs their pot of hoosh. Hayward sits staring at the hoosh, with nothing to say, and Richards' thoughts are limited: "The Skipper is very lame. I asked Tubby how Smithy is doing, and he said that he keeps pretty cheerful, and he doesn't howl much, like Tubby said he would."

None of the men are in good shape and Mackintosh is now hanging on to the sledge most of the time. When snow falls the going is very difficult as at times they are up to their knees in snow. On other days it is blowing and snowing so heavily they cannot even travel. Another factor adding to their distress is the light is getting murkier by the day, as the sun is now staying near the horizon, and this makes steering even more difficult. However, somehow, they manage to pick up their cairns, those laid on the way out to Mount Hope, and stay close to the correct route.

Joyce and Richards listen to Hayward speaking his thoughts out loud one early morning: "You know, I cannot help thinking what extraordinary things take place in the course of a man's otherwise ordinary existence."

"What things Vic?" asks Richards.

"Here am I at the uttermost end of the earth, lying in a fur bag, inside a little tent, with two other chaps, with a wind at 40 miles an hour and a temperature of 50 below outside, when I ought to be sitting in front of the fire at home and keeping warm."

Richards smiles, but he is more interested in their location, the distance to safety.

"And where are we now Vic?"

Hayward looks at his daily log of the distance travelled for the day.

"I think about 15 miles to the next depot, the Bluff Depot, so we are about 85 miles from Hut Point, but I fear we could be rather up against it."

However, at this stage, Joyce is still optimistic: "Dogs are still in splendid condition and going as well as ever. They're little marvels. At this rate we shall soon polish off the remainder."

***

They camp that next evening, February 17, as exhausted as they have been most days recently. Their progress that day was particularly slow and towards evening, with a low snow drift blowing, they had lost their line of cairns. They had lost them because they had 'carpet sweepers'; that is snow drift up to perhaps four or five feet. That day they had been going on a bearing which Richards thought was pretty right, but they were not on the line of cairns when they camped that night.

Richards is not anxious as he thinks he will be able to pick up the cairns again in the morning and none of the other men are worried either. They are close to the next depot, with its ample supply of provisions, and even Mackintosh is in a positive frame of mind.

He says to Spencer-Smith: "Hope to reach Bluff Depot tomorrow padre."

"Given light we should be Skipper. Domine Deus exaudi."

Wild is slightly more circumspect: "Let's hope God is listening but I'm very doubtful, as there are heavy clouds flying around."

They are only ten miles from a well-stocked depot and approximately 80 miles from the complete safety of Hut Point, and they still have provisions for a couple of days so there is not a great deal of concern. However, autumn is closing in. Their serious problems are about to begin.

CHAPTER 12

Move, or die like Scott

Four dogs curl up in the snow while six men doze in their sleeping bags. Incessant snow falls and a furious wind rages.

Conditions are too thick for travelling on the next day, so they decide to wait for the weather to clear. Except for an occasional peep at the howling 'pea soup' weather outside the six men hibernate and it is extraordinary how they sleep the time away. They feel a great sense of security inside the tent, but they are fully aware that only the thin canvas wall of the tent separates them from the cold, the misery, the discomfort and the danger outside.

They are unperturbed having to wait; with some thinking the enforced rest may even be of some benefit.

"One day's lay-up is against our grain," Joyce tells Richards and Hayward, "but it won't harm us, especially the Skipper. He is keeping up pretty fair, better than I expected."

Richards is intrigued by Joyce's life, so foreign to his own.

"When did you join the Navy?"

"When I was fifteen. As a young boy I was sent to a school for orphans to go in the Royal Navy. A tough school Richy, fifty of us sleeping in one dorm and thousands of us in a huge dining hall, parade drills every day. But at fifteen I was not smart enough for more than the bottom rank of the navy, as a boy second class seaman. After being with Scott I joined up with Shackleton on his *Nimrod* expedition."

"But you were not with him when he almost got to the Pole?"

"No. I was in charge of stocking the depots for his return trip, like we are doing now for Shacks. We always built large snow cairns, with bamboo poles and black flags so they could be found easily. I remember at one depot we left some luxuries; eggs, cakes, and plum pudding."

Hayward thinks that some luxuries would be welcome now. "We've only three days provisions left, and perhaps a gallon of kerosene to share with Mack's tent," he says.

Joyce is comfortable with these provisions: "This is ample on which to make the Bluff Depot, normally. But we'll follow our customary practice during lay ups and go onto two meals a day only."

"Two pots of hoosh between the three of us is fine," says Richards.

Joyce queries him: "What about the dogs Richie? What is left for them?"

"There are plenty of biscuits, enough for a few days."

Joyce reassures his companions: "The depot is close by and the weather should lift soon."

Hayward scribbles in his diary and turns to Richards: "Easy note today Rich. It is February 18 and we have travelled zero miles. There is still 80 miles to go to reach the hut."

The six men are on reduced rations, but the well-stocked Bluff Depot is nearby, and they believe they are only a week away from Hut Point. Richards is not concerned, and Joyce is quite optimistic that the blizzard which is holding them up will soon die down and allow them to move on.

***

"This blizzard almost carries a note of personal animus," says Spencer-Smith. It is a foreboding comment.

In their tent, Mackintosh, Wild and Spencer-Smith are in the same predicament as Joyce, Richards and Wild. The blizzard has now raged non-stop for three days, but the laconic Ernest Wild seems to have no concerns: "So, we are on one meal a day again, about the same place too."

"Going without meals keeps us colder," says Mackintosh. "There's no doubt food is the fuel in more ways than one."

On the following day Wild's quip to Spencer-Smith and Mackintosh is: "Still reducing rations. I'll have to make more holes in my belt."

They are living in pools of water made by their bodies lying in the same place for such a long time. There has been no chance of any travelling as it has been blowing continuously without a lull and by the fourth day of the blizzard their situation is becoming critical. They have no idea what they will do if the blizzard does not stop. Their daily ration is now down to a quarter of a pint of pemmican, to be shared amongst three, plus one biscuit and a few lumps of sugar. Then their cooking oil runs out, so they cannot even melt snow for a warm drink.

"We've plenty of tea," says Joyce, "but no ammunition to cook it with."

Pannikin.

However, Richards improvises. He pours some methylated spirit into a pannikin and lights it – the spirit was used to start the Primus cooker – and then places a pot of snow over the slow burning spirts. The snow melts lethargically, taking half an hour to melt enough for one pannikin.

Richards hands the shared pannikin of lukewarm tea to Joyce to have the first sip. "This is a very slow process, but it is the only way we can get a drink of something other than snow."

Joyce is now very concerned. "Things are getting serious. It's still blizzarding and the dog provisions are nearly out so we have to half their rations again."

"Let's hope for the best," says Hayward.

Their food is running out and Mackintosh and Spencer-Smith's health is not improving. They have no fuel for the cookers, and the dogs are weakening because they have had little food for four days.

***

"Frizzled bacon and eggs," says Mackintosh.

"Lamb chops and chipped potatoes," are the thoughts that come to Wild's mind.

"And coffee Wild. Imagine how that would go down."

Spencer-Smith joins the conversation, on the food they would love to be eating.

"I'm not particularly hungry for some reason, but I keep thinking of new milk, creamy butter and cheese."

"What about some porridge and toast and butter Wild?" says Mackintosh.

"Yes Skipper, and some new brown bread, and jam."

Spencer-Smith smiles: "I wonder why newly laid eggs and pickles intrude into my dream meals?"

Suddenly there appears to be a lull in the weather, so Wild clambers out of his bag, but as soon as he looks out heavy snow starts falling again. Outside he sees a scene of chaos where the howling wind is whirling the snow around, obliterating everything. The dogs are completely buried, and only a mound with a ski sticking up indicates where the sledge is. The six men long to be on the move, but the howling of the wind tells them how impossible that is.

Wild returns to the tent to find the other two, Mackintosh and Spencer-Smith, snoring peacefully so he lies down too, toggles up his sleeping bag and courts sleep, which eventually comes. The sleeping-bags are damp and sticky inside, but fortunately, at this time in late February, the temperature is 'relatively' high – between minus 10 and minus 20 Fahrenheit – so the insides of the bags do not freeze if they are in them.

Mackintosh wakes and mutters at Wild.

"What a place, still, what else can we expect? It's all happened before and we knew it would be so before we came so we must grin and bear it."

***

"This blizzard has to stop, otherwise we'll be sharing the fate of Scott and his party," says a worried Joyce.

Their position on the Great Ice Barrier is ominously close to where

Captain Scott and two of his men perished. In March of 1912, Scott, Wilson and Bowers were camped just 11 miles from their next food depot, the One Ton Depot, which was at latitude 79° 30' S. The six men of the Mount Hope Party are camped 10 miles from their next food depot, the Minna Bluff Depot, near latitude 79° S. They all know how Scott died.

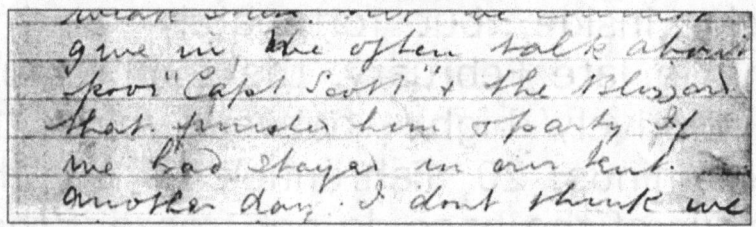

Joyce diary page – we often talk about poor Capt. Scott and the blizzard that finished him. Courtesy of Betsy Krementz.

In the tent, the men now think of Scott quite often; they cannot help but think of him as their location and predicament is so similar. Richards raises the topic openly: "I don't want to die like Scott. I think he lost his resolve to travel and so he died in his tent. If the blizzard doesn't stop, we'll just have to make the effort to reach our depot."

Joyce knows that scurvy has taken hold on them all, and he also knows that one of the effects of scurvy is to lose one's willpower. Richards continues to speak his thoughts out loud.

"You know, it's very easy to die. We could just lie here and just let it happen."

"You are not thinking of dying here Richie, are you?" asks Hayward.

"No. I've no thought of dying, it just seems an easy thing to do, in this sort of situation."

He goes on: "But we have to do something as I think the food for the dogs has almost run out. We have no food. For us, there is just one emergency meal of pemmican which we'll use just before we start again."

Joyce realises they will have to make a move: "I gave the dogs the last of their food tonight. We'll have to push on soon as a great deal depends on them."

Richards agrees, and puts forward a suggestion: "Let's get underway tomorrow. Whatever the weather is like."

"I wonder how the others are doing." Hayward asks.

"Impossible to talk to them, with that howling wind," says Joyce.

Richards holds up his hand: "Listen. I can hear a burst of song from Tubby, so they're in the land of the living."

Hayward hears Wild as well. "He has just called out that he has just eaten his meal for the day, and it was two biscuits and a chunk of snow."

The blizzard surpasses in length and fury anything Joyce has experienced. It is impossible to see or communicate with the other tent because of the howling of the wind and the snow is now almost covering their tent, so they think that even exiting may be difficult. The drift has banked up against the frail walls and is gradually restricting the space inside, so their three sleeping bags are cramped together side by side. Hour after monotonous hour is spent in them as the hours and days slowly pass by, but they find real rest impossible.

The six men are spending an inordinate amount of time simply lying in their sleeping bags, and missing meals, so they are starting to feel the cold more and more every day. Richards lies there and he notices it is his feet that are the first to show signs of cold after a warm pannikin of tea. Then the cold gradually works its way up his body. After about eight hours from when he last had a warm drink, he begins to feel an urgent need for food, or at least another pannikin of tea, to warm his body a little.

But the blizzard roars on. Joyce, Richards and Hayward talk the matter over again and they know the six of them have to make the effort and get under way. They realise they just have to march, no matter what risk of disaster might be involved, even though the wind and drift are still as violent as ever. Under normal circumstances they would not even contemplate travelling.

***

On the morning of the sixth day of the blizzard, Joyce notices a slight lull in the wind. He yells out: "She's breaking!"

There is no response from the other tent, so he calls out again, to

Mackintosh: "Sir. We should shift as soon as we've had a meal."

Fortunately, the weather has eased slightly. They see a break in the clouds, so they decide to eat the last meal they had kept just for this situation, before getting under way. Mackintosh enquires whether Joyce, Richards and Hayward have any pemmican to spare, but they have none. Wild tells Joyce that he, Mackintosh and Spencer-Smith have none either, just a bag of oatmeal, some Bovril cubes, one bag of chocolate and some biscuits, so they are slightly better off. The six men have something to eat, but not the dogs. There's no food for them.

Outside they find the wind has hardly abated and it is still snowing heavily, so it takes Joyce, Richards and Hayward over two hours to dig out their sledge. They quickly discover that they are very weak. They have great difficulty in doing anything – with just two digs of the shovel they are out of breath – caused by their laying up for six days and having very little food.

"Richie, I must say that I have never experienced such weakness in my life," yells Hayward across the howling of the wind.

They stow everything on the sledge; the two tents, five sleeping bags, and other items and then Wild carries Spencer-Smith forward – still in his sleeping bag – and places him on top of everything. They lash him to the sledge but then the wind increases in intensity, and the snow falls become heavier.

Mackintosh calls out.

"I do not think we can march in these conditions."

Richards is not impressed with Mackintosh's reluctance to make a move.

"Mack, we must march. Joycey, Vic, Tubby and I, and the four dogs, can still pull. We have to make a start today."

Mackintosh calls out again: "I'm unable to walk."

"Tie yourself alongside the sledge Sir," yells Joyce. "Ease your weight by it."

After some more persuasion from Joyce and Richards, Mackintosh agrees to make the effort to move on. Richards thinks that Mackintosh seems to have lost all initiative and has acquiesced to him and Joyce taking over leadership of the party. With Spencer-Smith tied to the top of the sledge, they set off, but the five men and the four dogs are much weaker now than when they halted six days earlier.

Richards looks around, and it is a pathetic sight, not a lot more than a total scene of whirling snow, where there is a sort of milky whiteness over everything. The snow is falling on Joyce, who Richards can just see ahead at the end of a rope, it is falling over the four dogs following Joyce, and over all the men. Wild and Hayward are tied to the sledge, straining forward. Spencer-Smith is lashed to the sledge in his sleeping bag and protected as far as they can manage from the wind and snow. Mackintosh teeters along, holding on to the sledge at its rear.

They find the snow surface to be extremely soft and deep so the sledge bogs at frequent intervals, and in their weak state it is as much as the four fitter men, and the dogs, can do to restart her. Fortunately, the dogs, even though they have been on short rations for some days, work splendidly.

The next depot, the Minna Bluff Depot, is less than ten miles away, but the weather is incredible. The men cannot see anything, and with the howling wind they find it difficult to even stay on their feet. They simply lurch along with the wind buffeting everything.

After only an hour, where they cover less than a mile, Mackintosh sits down and cries out: "I can't go any further, I've got to stop."

Richards yells at him: "Don't be a bloody fool."

Mackintosh cries out again: "Oh my hands, my hands."

Hayward calls out for the dogs to halt and Joyce goes back to Mackintosh.

"Joyce, I can't go any further. Just wrap me up in a deck cloth let me lie here in the snow. My legs are swollen black."

"Let me have a look at your gums, Sir." Joyce sees they are black.

"I think you have got scurvy Sir."

Spencer-Smith hears them talking and asks Hayward what is happening.

"The Skipper has declared himself done up and is unable to proceed."

"You know, he has for weeks been suffering from a strained knee and bleeding from the bowels," says Spencer-Smith.

Joyce, Richards, Hayward and Wild discuss the situation, and they make a momentous decision. They decide – quickly – that Mackintosh and Spencer-Smith will have to stay while some of the others push on to the next depot. They realise it is essential that a fit man be left to look after the two sick men, and as Wild had been looking after Spencer-Smith the obvious course to follow seems to be for Wild to stay with them. Joyce, Richards and Hayward are a compact party and feel they should go on. They can promise Wild nothing more than they will head off and see what they can do; hopefully reach the Bluff Depot and bring back food.

Wild says nothing. Richards is sure Wild does not like the idea of being left behind, and he knows that he would have felt the same.

Joyce and Richards then have a brief conversation with Mackintosh. They tell him they will put the tent up and he will stay with Spencer-Smith and Wild. Mackintosh listens but he too says nothing and to Richards, he doesn't seem to be all there, mentally. They make Mackintosh and Spencer-Smith as comfortable as possible and leave practically all the food with Wild and these two sick men; some biscuits, four cubes of Bovril, and a little tea.

As soon as Joyce, Richards and Hayward and the four dogs – Oscar, Con, Towser and Gunner – start to move off, it begins to snow heavily. After a few moments Richards looks back but the tent with Mackintosh, Spencer-Smith and Wild has already disappeared.

He doubts he will ever see these three men again.

With the blizzard showing no signs of easing, Richards, Joyce and Hayward have decided to make a dash to reach the next depot. Wild is staying with the ailing Mackintosh and the incapacitated Spencer-Smith. Their fate is in now the hands of the three men who have just left them, who have virtually no food and little fuel to even heat water for a pannikin of tea. The dogs have no food at all. The fate of Wild, Spencer-Smith and Mackintosh Survival depends entirely on the will to live of Joyce, Richards and Hayward.

CHAPTER 13

Navigating in white out conditions

Sketch of the dogs with Richards and Hayward.

Richards finds that the heel of his leading foot is never placed beyond the toe of the other. With each step he, and Joyce and Hayward, gain two or three inches at most and sometimes they even lose what they have gained with back-slipping. At other times, when snow is up to their waists, Richards feels like they are doing little more than marking time.

Lack of visibility is an even more significant problem. They can only see a few yards and the sky is no different in appearance to anywhere else. There appears to be no up or down and with zero visibility they have extreme difficulty in steering, like they are walking into a blank wall. North is the same as south.

They are attempting to find and follow the course along the line of cairns that had been placed when they went out to Mount Hope, but they do not know where the line is. They had lost them the day before the blizzard started. Richards knows the bearings of the line of cairns, they are in his diary having been taken on the way out, but he does not know if they are to his right or the left. However, he knows that if he keeps Joyce on the known bearings, they would remain roughly parallel to the line of cairns and be close to the right course towards the Bluff Depot.

Richards and Joyce work together, as they had before when trying to steer in a blizzard. Joyce is on the end of a long rope and Richards takes a bearing to set Joyce on the right line. However, bearings are not easy to take for Richards because he has to get his hands out of his mitts to hold the aluminium compass. It is a painful business in the cold, with bare fingers, and he can only manage to hold the metal of the compass for a couple of seconds before he has to put it away and put his mitts on again.

After giving Joyce the direction with the rope they judge the wind, which is often coming from the south-east over their right shoulders, and try to maintain that same course, based solely on the direction of the wind. They can see nothing ahead but a white featureless void, nothing at all to guide them to keep a straight course. In the circumstances, trying to navigate by the wind direction is the best they can do. It is all they can do; watching the way the rope lay in reference to the wind and try to maintain that angle.

They only go on for a short time, about a quarter or half an hour and then halt where Richards takes another reading and adjusts Joyce's direction. They push for another 15 minutes or so and repeat the process, again, and again.

***

"It will be a cup of warm tea," says Richards, "if I can coax the metho to light. Normally it goes up like that when you put a match to it, but down here in the cold it's so bloody hard to light. It just won't."

Joyce knows he will not be drinking a steaming hot pannikin of tea: "Throw a few tea leaves in Richie when you have some warm water. That'll have to do."

Joyce, Richards and Hayward are at camp on the first evening after leaving the others, and they have what they call their banquet: a cup of warm tea and half a biscuit. The howling blizzard had continued all day and into the evening. They estimate they have travelled at a rate of a half to three-quarters of a mile per hour, so guess they have covered about three miles, but without their sledge-meter they do not really know.

To Richards, the situation does not look particularly cheerful. He and the other two are very weak and feel the effects of the six-day lay-up. He lies in his cold wet sleeping bag in the dark, as they are now losing the sun for four hours a day. Joyce's snoring tells him he is a deep sleep, but Richards finds it impossible – for some cause or causes unknown – to sleep a wink.

In the morning he sees Hayward once again scribbling notes in his diary, and on this morning, Richards also starts keeping a diary.

"Why the note taking now Rich?" asks Hayward.

"I simply want to make a record of what has gone on. I am troubled that we have left the others behind. I have doubts that we will even find the Minna Bluff Depot and even if we do, I have no idea whether we will ever see Mack, Smithy and Tubby again."

Richards has watched both Hayward and Joyce make diary entries on most days, with Joyce in particular making meticulous notes of what went on during the day. He knew that Joyce tended to exaggerate at times, or 'draw the long bow' or even embroider the truth a bit at times, so he wanted to put down his views on exactly what had happened, without any embellishment.

***

Breakfast is a pannikin of tepid tea and one biscuit, shared between three men, but there is nothing for the dogs. It is three hours from waking before Joyce, Richards and Hayward can get underway; mainly because of the time it takes the methylated spirits to melt some snow for their tea.

Once again, conditions are horrendous, but the three men and the four dogs labour on. Every time the sledge hits a snow drift, she becomes stuck in it, although there is only 200 pounds on board, and then, in spite of the efforts of the three men and four dogs, they can only shift her with a "1-2-3 haul". After five hours of hauling in the morning, in a blinding snowstorm, they stop and put up the tent for their lunch. They hope they have covered another three miles that morning.

For lunch they eat a quarter of a biscuit each.

"As meagre as breakfast," says Hayward, "and we are now almost completely out of food."

Joyce has an idea: "You know, with some scrapings from the dog-tank I might be able to get us a scanty meal."

The dog-tank is a canvas bag in which they kept the dog pemmican, so they scrape it for crumbs and anything else left there to try and get some sort of nutrient. They mix this with warm water but when they come to drink it, they cannot stomach it. Joyce can only swallow a mouthful or two, Richards almost chokes on it and Hayward, after smelling it, cannot even bring himself to have a sip. It is the worst tasting meal they have ever tried to eat.

Their problems then multiply. Their tent is one of Scott's old tents and a few small rips have appeared, and they are desperately frightened that the steam from the cooking that freezes on the tent will induce one of the rips to tear completely.

And, just as they are ready to resume early in the afternoon, before they are able to pull down the tent and stow it on the sledge, the wind comes up from the south-west. It is so violent and accompanied by such snow that they are driven back into the tent, which fortunately they had not struck. They are able to get their sleeping bags into the tent, with themselves and the bags covered with snow. After some difficulty they manage to spread the bags and struggle inside them.

"That wind force is about 70 to 80," says Joyce.

Hayward shivers: "I feel so cold."

"Lack of food Vic," Joyce tells him. "It allows the cold to do its worst with us."

Hayward is dispirited: "How often at home have I seen people stick their hands into these self-same sleeping bags and say 'That's all right. How could you get cold in that?' But then they were dry, and therein lies the secret of sleeping bag comfort."

"That's right Vic," says Joyce. "Find a way of keeping the sleeping bag dry and you will defy any cold."

"But how to do it?" asks Hayward. "Snow creeps in in minute quantities no matter how careful I am. Moisture from my breathing condenses and freezes, and the snow and ice accumulate."

"I reckon," adds Joyce," that perhaps within a fortnight, our bags would have doubled in weight."

The wind does not stop until seven o'clock that evening, so they quickly turn out, but find it is snowing so thickly and the light is so poor that it is impossible to proceed. They can see nothing in any direction and realise it would be folly to proceed as no course could be steered. In addition, they are very weak, so they go back into the tent, lie down in their sleeping bags and mark time.

"All we can do is wait for a lull in conditions," says Joyce, "and urgent as the need is, we can't face this."

Hayward is very disconsolate: "This is going to be very difficult."

Richards knows the condition of the dogs is paramount: "The worst of camping is the poor dogs. This is the second day they've been without any food and if we can't save the dogs it will be almost impossible to drag our two invalids back."

Joyce is fearful: "If they crack up it will be very serious."

As is Hayward: "I think we are in a very bad case. We are now practically without food and any way of heating. We've no means of telling how far we are from the depot. In fact, it seems to me, taking everything into consideration that it is going to be a very close call indeed."

"Think of Scott and the blizzard that finished him and his party," says Richards. "We must keep moving. If we stay in our tent here another day, I don't think we'll ever get under way at all."

But Hayward continues with his pessimist attitude. "I am about all in. I am sure that unless the weather changes for the better immediately there is little hope of us getting in."

Dramatically, Joyce tells them: "We must carry on, and die in the harness."

***

Sketch of Richards outside the tent.

In the morning, Richards struggles out to look at the weather.

"How does it look?" Joyce calls out.

"As thick as Hell. Snow and wind again."

Their third day away from the others turns out to be horribly similar to previous days. They get underway, once again halting every ten minutes or quarter of an hour to rest, and for Richards to check the direction Joyce is taking. It is snowing and blowing in much the same manner as the days before, but they manage to cover about three miles in the morning.

Richards watches the dogs carefully and although they now have little on the sledge, they seem to have lost their spirit. Three are losing heart, but the massive one, Oscar, appears to lower his head and pull as he never did when things were going well. At times he gets a little run on the sledge and tries to bite the heels of the dog ahead to make him work. They have been without any food for some days now and it seems to Richards that Oscar is aware that they are looking for something that would give him a full meal once more.

They stop for their lunch at noon, when it is snowing more heavily than ever, and by 2.30pm they have managed to obtain a warm cup of tea. They hope to then proceed but once again they cannot travel because the snow has become thicker than ever and is accompanied by a fierce wind.

Even Joyce sounds despondent now: "If anyone were to see us, they would be surprised. Three men staggering on with four dogs, with practically an empty sledge and just crawling along."

"We could eat the dogs," says Hayward, "for our own survival."

Richards does not agree. "But it wouldn't save our lives Vic. Without them we wouldn't even reach the Bluff Depot. Let's discard that idea."

"Richie is right Vic. Even if we eat only one dog, we would be signing our own death warrant. We can't make any progress without the help of four dogs."

The tent is becoming even more of a worry, as it is now badly torn in the front and they are afraid to move on account of the tear; that it might split open the whole tent. It is too cold outside to mend it, so they hope to make the depot before they are forced to pitch it again.

Richards is reluctant to move, but for a different reason; he does not want to travel on because he does not know where they stand in regard to the depot. He believes they may have travelled nine or ten miles since leaving Mackintosh, Spencer-Smith and Wild, but with the thick weather he feels they may have strayed from the course of the cairns. He has no idea as to where the depot lies.

"Look there's no use going on," he says to Joyce and Hayward. "We might as well wait here and see what happens. By my rough reckoning of distance, I believe that to go further might put us beyond the depot. We may have already passed it and the worst thing would be to overshoot the depot."

***

Richards cannot sleep. It is another unspeakable night, with regards to the weather, and he knows they are in a critical situation. They are now completely without food and this day may be their last, if they do not reach the depot. At about 2am he goes outside and finds it clearing. It is light enough to see, so they pack up.

They travel for less than an hour, and then Richards spots the depot. They had camped no more than three quarters of a mile from it, but could not see it on the previous day, because of the thick weather. The dogs see the depot too and it electrifies them. They suddenly have a new lease of life and start to run but Joyce, Richards and Hayward are so weak they cannot go more than a few yards without a spell.

"You did it Richie", says Joyce. "You laid the course."

"I don't know how I did it, I really don't know."

"The depot, finally," says Hayward. "I can't describe how I feel. I am absolutely played out, but thankful indeed."

Joyce knows how close to death they were: "I think another day would have seen us off."

After a hard struggle they erect their tent and make camp, and their first job is to give the dogs a good feed of pemmican. Joyce is full of praise for the dogs.

"If ever dogs saved the lives of anyone, they've saved ours. Let's hope they continue in good health so that we can get out to Mack and the others."

Joyce, Richards and Hayward now know they are in clover, because they can eat as much they like. The depot has a substantial supply of fuel and sledging rations, although there is no fresh meat to alleviate their scurvy. They decide to rest up and recover before heading back to pick up Mackintosh, Spencer-Smith and Wild, and also to give the dogs a few meals. They know it might be fatal to send them out too soon, and the lives of their three companions depend on the dogs being healthy. In addition, the rips in their tent have to be repaired before they start back.

Joyce starts cooking some pemmican, but surprisingly, neither he, Richards or Hayward has any appetite for it, so Joyce heats up some rolled oats with powdered milk for a start, which they do consume.

Joyce is not on edge anymore: "How cheery the Primus sounds. It seems like we have come out of a thick London fog into a drawing room."

They fix the tent rips using a canvas food bag, with Joyce sewing from the inside and Richards on the outside. Then they rest and eat several very light meals, but at fairly short intervals. They pack the sledge, planning to head back south early the next morning, and take the precaution of attaching a second sledge, knowing they will probably have to haul back Mackintosh as well as Spencer-Smith.

Hayward is despondent that there is no news at the Bluff Depot about the

Aurora: "Which needless to say is not exactly cheering," he says.

"No. Very sad," says Joyce. "Stevens was going to leave a message here."

Richards is pessimistic: "I fear she has gone down probably with all hands."

Hayward knows his health is deteriorating and he is now gloomier than ever: "I am sure the ship has not returned."

Joyce thinks there could have been something left at the depot by the three men who returned in early January: "And not even anything here from Cope, Jack or Gaze. I guess they got back to the Cape Evans hut okay and are with Stevens."

Even though these three men have plenty of food, uppermost on their minds is that they still have to reach the safety of Hut Point. They have another 90 miles to go. Ten miles to go back and pick up the other three men and then 80 from there to Hut Point, and they know it will be a very hard 90 miles. Joyce is also worried about his health, as he is being troubled by weakness and shortness of breath, but he hopes this will pass in due course, now he is back onto full rations.

As they load up the sledge with provisions, Richards notices that Hayward cannot straighten his legs. In the evening he asks Hayward if he can look at them. They are blue and black at the back, so Richards rubs methylated spirits on them. Hayward's condition is worse than Joyce or Richards, although they too have some stiffness and discoloration behind the knees. Hayward knows he has been getting weaker and has tried to be cheerful, but he is realising that he may not be able to walk for much longer.

After fighting the blizzard for three days, Richards, Joyce and Hayward have covered the ten miles to the depot. They are now safe, but their next task is to head back south to try and find their three companions. From this time on, Hayward becomes a less and less effective unit in the party.

CHAPTER 14

Waiting, and hoping

Richards is apprehensive: "This is awful. We cannot even start, held up here at the Bluff knowing the others are starving and worse deathly cold, ten or so miles back."

A strong blizzard is blowing preventing them from heading back to rescue Mackintosh, Spencer-Smith and Wild. Hayward is as concerned as Richards: "Beastly Richie. Perfectly beastly."

A hurricane wind and heavy snow has greeted Joyce, Richards and Hayward at 5am and it is impossible to see anything outside, so they sit on their rolled up sleeping bags, and wait.

"This is the longest blizzard I've ever been in," says Joyce. "We've not had a travelling day for 11 days."

Richards goes outside to feed the dogs, but the tent entrance is blocked with snow and he has a hard job to even get out. Outside he cannot see the dogs or the sledge as they are completely buried. He can only tell where they are by their round breathing holes.

The weather breaks at 10am and by noon they ready to start on their way, in a southerly direction once again. However, they cannot move the sledge even though it is very light. All they have on board are items like their tent, their sleeping bags, cooking items, three weeks' food and enough dog-food, although they are towing an extra sledge. Joyce estimates the whole weight being no more than 600 pounds.

They clean the sledge runners, and this makes hauling a little easier, but the dogs are unsettled and engage in a pitched battle shortly after starting. The three men are absolutely exhausted when at last they are able to separate them. The dogs are crucial to their efforts to return and save the three other men, but the dogs do not want to go back south. Richards thinks they seem to know instinctively they are going the wrong way. However, by driving them north at first and then slowly working them around to the south, they get underway. The men see that the dogs have lost all heart in pulling, as though going south again is not good for them. They seem to just jog along, and all the whipping in the world makes no impression on them.

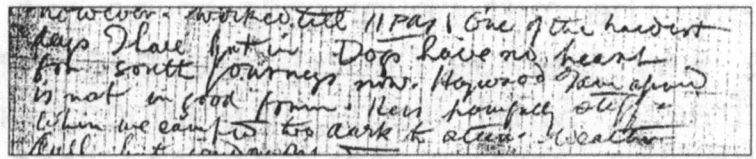

Richards diary note February 27, 1916—Dogs have no heart...—courtesy David L. Harrowfield.

Hayward can hardly walk now, so it is Joyce and Richards and the four dogs that do the majority of the hauling. They stop at 11pm when it is too dark to steer, thinking they have covered about five and a half miles. That night, they are too tired and too disconsolate to talk a lot.

After their meal of hoosh Richards spends an hour or so in rubbing Hayward's legs with methylated spirits, which helps him considerably, but Hayward is quite despondent: "For my part I felt I could not have gone much further tonight."

"If you break up Vic," says Joyce. "We don't know what we will do."

The light at night is a sort of visible darkness. Every time they put down a mitt to open a food bag or tie one up the mitt somehow disappears, through an inconsiderate movement of one of them. The mitt never fails to be out of the way just as fingers are beginning to freeze. Small items, like spoons and pannikins, remain lost until the tent is vacated the next morning because the cold is so intense, and they are very wary of looking for things without their mitts on. Even with their mitts on it is difficult to tell what they have hold of, in the dark, as it is almost impossible to diagnose the shape.

That night, like most nights now for Richards, he does not know if he has any sleep at all. The night seems interminable and he rises unrefreshed.

***

Their pace on the next day is slower, estimated by Joyce to be a half or three-quarters of a mile per hour. The surface is rotten, snow is up to their knees, and there is a head wind, plus heavy snow is falling. The weather is so thick they are unable to pick up their cairns and Richards has to direct Joyce in the same hit or miss fashion they used on the journey to the depot.

They manage to travel for three hours in the morning before the blizzard comes on again. Richards tells Joyce it would be folly to proceed further as he reckons by the number of hours they have marched that they are somewhere in the vicinity of the others. They stay in their tent and Richards looks out at intervals to see if anything can be seen. He knows the others must be nearby, but he cannot see very far.

They wait. The wind continues to blow, and heavy snow continues to fall, but they keep a look out for a break which might allow them to locate the others, who they think must be within a mile. Hayward writes in his diary that it is impossible to describe his feelings in this matter. He makes a note that he, Joyce and Richards are waiting to help their three companions but have no idea where they are.

Richards frets: "I am distraught. To be within reach of the others but prevented from rendering aid on account of the thick weather."

He even goes outside and shouts, in the remote hope that they could be nearby. Back inside the tent he says to Joyce and Hayward: "I fear what we may find on arriving. I keep wondering how it will all end."

***

"Tubby, you are just like Mrs Micawber, staying to look after the Skipper and me."

Wild smiles. He has no idea what Spencer-Smith is talking about.

"She is a Charles Dickens character named Emma, and she's the wife of a Mr. Micawber. It is in the book David Copperfield and Emma was a long suffering wife but she swears she'll never leave him, despite his financial difficulties."

Wild smiles again.

"Well padre, you and the Skipper are both unwell, so someone has to be with you. Joyce, Richie and I had a bit of a palaver and we all agreed that I was the one to stay."

"I expect to see them back here in three or four days," says Mackintosh.

"I've no complaints," says Wild.

Mackintosh, Spencer-Smith and Wild can do nothing but wait – and hope – for the return Joyce, Richards and Hayward from the Minna Bluff Depot. Understandably, they talk about little else but the weather, and where the others might be. The strong winds and heavy snow continue after Joyce, Richards and Hayward leave, so they know they have probably not travelled very far that first afternoon. On the second day they see the sun shining and it is quite calm in the location of their tent so they think the other party may have then reached the depot. On the third day the wind is blowing worse than ever and it is snowing all the time, but Wild hopes it is the final blow before it clears. On the next day it is calm where they are, and Wild clears the tent front, after burrowing his way out through a great mass of snow drift at the tent door. Then, to help guide the others back he builds a large cairn and puts some black bunting on it, because their tent now only shows about a foot above the snow.

By day five they anticipate that the others will be back some time on the following day. On the morning of their sixth day it is calm but then, to their great disappointment, everything becomes obscured by falling snow, so no help arrives. At this time Joyce, Richards and Hayward are camped close by.

The other preoccupation of Mackintosh, Spencer-Smith and Wild is food. They were left with very little; a small number of biscuits, a few sticks of chocolate, and a few oddments such as dried vegetables, Bovril and lime juice tablets. They had 'two meals' of cooking fuel but after the fuel runs out, Wild makes up a methylated spirits cooker. They then move onto what they call 'tiddly meals', twice daily, consisting of a few thinly sliced vegetables which they have with a Bovril cube. The occasional cup of tea warms them up, and they revel in it.

"What a great and glorious cup of tea," Spencer-Smith calls it.

"I wish we had cocoa padre," says Mackintosh. "I find the tea to be beastly rotten as the only taste we get is hotness and wetness."

As they start to run low on food, Wild retains his sense of humour, calling their scanty meals 'dishy feeds' and that he will have to take after a 'Yankee fasting man' if the others don't appear soon. By the sixth day they are down to their last meal of rations, two very scratch meals, and Wild says to the others: "My belly is singing Rule Britannia."

Wild diary note February 27, 1916—... my belly is singing Rule Britannia now—courtesy David L. Harrowfield.

***

Mackintosh reads the final words in Scott's Journal, 'For God's sake look after our people'.

He then writes: 'Goodbye friends. I feel sure our people, my own dear wife and children will not be neglected.'

Mackintosh is in his sleeping bag, writing a long note and from the sentiment of his words it seems like he is looking over his shoulder at an unseen audience. He believes he may soon die, like Scott. He has the book titled *Scott's Last Expedition,* which had been published in England before Mackintosh left. It is an edited version of Scott's diaries.

In his long note Mackintosh explains the plight of him and his men, and that he is not a hundred percent confident that help will come. He attempts to exonerate himself from any blame, writing in positive terms of their efforts and in particular Wild's behaviour. He acknowledges that he and Spencer-Smith succumbed to scurvy before the others, because of a lack of fresh food.

Many of Mackintosh's written words have an eerie similarity to those that Scott wrote as he lay dying in his tent in March 1912.

Scott had written: 'It would do your heart good to be in our tent, to hear our songs and the cheery conversation as to what we will do when we get to Hut Point.'

And Mackintosh writes: 'We have not given up hope yet by any means, we trust in our comrades. We argue, say – talk cheery today and anyone coming along would imagine to be some picnic party.'

Scott had written: 'We have no cause for complaint, but bow to the will of Providence, determined still to do our best to the last ... which would have stirred the heart of every Englishman.'

And Mackintosh writes: 'But I leave it on record all have done their duty nobly & well. This is all I can say and if it is God's will that we should here give up we do so in the true British fashion my own tradition holds us in power to do.'

Mackintosh writes a letter to his brother George, again with striking similarities to Scott's letter to an old friend J.M. Barrie.

Mackintosh writes: 'My dear old George, Well old man it's come to this – at least it looks like it. That I have to say farewell to my kith and kin, to peg out in this God-forsaken hole ... I know you will have a watchful eye on my ones...'

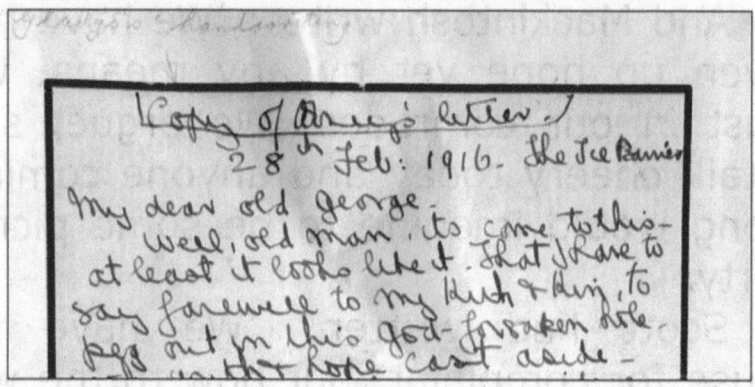

Mackintosh letter February 28, 1915-My dear old George, well, old man, its come to this – courtesy Canterbury Museum, Christchurch, New Zealand.

Scott had written: 'My Dear Barrie, We are pegging out in a very comfortless spot. Hoping this letter may be found and sent to you, I write a word of farewell.... More practically I want you to help my widow and my boy--your godson.'

While Wild prepares their minuscule meals and carries out tasks like clearing away snow from the entrance to their tent, Mackintosh and Spencer-Smith do little but lie in their damp and sticky clothes inside their wet sleeping bags.

The bags freeze if they are not lying inside them.

Conditions are truly abhorrent, day and night. They have a pannikin of warm tea or Bovril and then with half-frozen fingers they toggle themselves up inside their sleeping bags. As they lie there, they hear ice on the tent crackling and then drops of thawing ice fall on their faces. It is worse at night when it is dark and very cold in the tent, and as the night wears on the temperature drops and they start to shiver. A puddle of water forms underneath their body and their sleeping bags are ice cold on top. They doze off now and again but only for an hour or two at a time.

On their sixth day Wild is pragmatic as always.

"Another day gone and also all the scraps," he says.

Spencer-Smith remains positive: "I'm not downhearted, yet. God's in His Heaven!"

As is Mackintosh: "I have not given up hope yet by any means."

But he is dispirited: "What on earth does one come to these parts of the earth? Is it worth the candle? Here we are frostbitten in the day and frozen at nights. No sleep. What a life!"

***

Richards looks around but he sees nothing; nothing but a Godforsaken milky white emptiness. He keeps staring searchingly through the falling snow. It is the morning of the seventh day after he, Joyce and Hayward had left Mackintosh, Spencer-Smith and Wild and the weather started clearing so they rolled up their sleeping bags and sat on them inside the tent. Richards went outside, straining to see some semblance of a tent.

Then, suddenly, he calls out: "I think I see something black."

He feels confident he can see a dark speck to the south, and he can; it is the black bunting on a cairn that Wild has put up, next to the tent. Richards knows the three of them have accomplished something that at times had seemed quite impossible.

It takes them a few hours to reach the other camp and when Wild hears them coming he comes out of the tent.

Joyce, Richards and Hayward give him a loud cheer. Wild then puts on his canvas harness and walks out to meet them, calling out that Mackintosh and Spencer-Smith are both alright. He ties his harness onto their sledge and helps them pull it the last short distance. Wild does this without any emotion or fanfare. He simply wants to give them a hand in.

Sketch of Wild greeting the returning men.

The young man Richards is astounded. He sees that this action by Wild is simply incredible and he is not sure how to define it: it is more than courage, possibly just spirit. He reckons that nine out of ten men would have simply stood at the door of the tent and said 'Thank God'.

He and Hayward are both overcome with emotion at Wild's actions and finding the three men still alive. They both break down and cry.

***

Mackintosh staggers out of tent: "I want to thank you for saving our lives."

"How are you all?" asks Joyce.

"We've no food left," replies Mackintosh.

"And Smithy's condition hasn't improved," says Wild.

Mackintosh, Spencer-Smith and Wild have waited a week for the return of Richards, Joyce and Hayward and finally they have arrived. The six men are back together, but now Hayward is also faltering with scurvy. After a quick meal, Mackintosh is encouraged to go ahead with the aid of a stick whilst the others stow the sledges. When they lift Spencer-Smith up they find he is in a hole about two feet deep, which his body has melted. In their weakened condition, and it takes the combined efforts of Wild, Joyce and Richards to lift him onto the sledge.

They soon overtake Mackintosh, who is struggling gamely but he can hardly stand so they put him in his sleeping bag on the back sledge and the four of them – Joyce, Richards, Hayward and Wild – plus the four dogs, somehow manage to haul the whole load, much to their surprise. They thought they may have had to relay, but Oscar, Con, Towser and Gunner are pulling splendidly, now they are on the home trail.

They camp that evening, but even though they have not even reached the Minna Bluff Depot, all of them, especially Mackintosh, Spencer-Smith and Wild, are full of joy.

"Full belly once more," says Wild, relishing his feed of hoosh.

Mackintosh is clearly delighted: "I think seeing them was the most welcome sight I have ever seen."

Spencer-Smith admits how fortunate they were: "We've had the closest of close calls – Deus det-incrementum."

In their tent, Joyce congratulates Richards: "We did it Richie.

We are back together, and all still alive."

"I was overjoyed when the weather cleared this morning," says Hayward, "and then to see their camp. You spotted something just to the south of us Rich."

"I could not see what it was at first. It was just a dark spot."

Hayward laughs: "And it took us considerably longer than we had anticipated to reach it. Such heavy going."

Richards is still taken by the actions of Wild that day: "What a great chap is Tubby, helping us like that. At this time, he and Mack and Smithy had been without food for some time."

"And we had been eating food for three days by then," says Hayward.

"Yes. Coming out to give us a hand. I broke down."

"Me too Richie."

Richards admits he was pessimistic: "I thought that Smith would be dead as he was pretty weak when we left them. I thought it was possible that he'd slipped his cable."

Hayward smiles at Richards' choice of words:" Mack was very weak too and he could only crawl out of the tent, and then he just staggered around."

But Joyce gives his Skipper some praise: "At least he could hobble a bit, with the aid of two sticks."

"Anyway, it was a marvel a few days before that we even found the depot," replies Richards. "Such a small speck to find in that blizzard. And then on the return journey we found the even smaller dot in this wilderness, their tent."

"It was you steering me," says Joyce.

"A fluke, Joycey, just a fluke."

CHAPTER 15

Scurvy

Sketch of dogs and men pulling sledge with sail up.

The young Australian Richard Richards, the Antarctic veteran Ernest

Joyce, and the ailing Victor Hayward have saved Mackintosh, Spencer-Smith and Wild. However, the six men still have around 80 miles to travel, to reach the safety of the *Discovery* hut at Hut Point. There they would find seals for fresh meat, which will cure their scurvy, and save Spencer-Smith's life.

At times they set up a sail, where they make good progress. They are conscious of the fact that without an assisting wind, which allows them to use the sail; they may not survive. Sometimes the wind is so strong the sledges overrun the men and dogs, and the men jump on board. However, the number of miles gained each day starts to diminish. On the first day after being reunited they manage 10 miles, but after a few more days they are making not much more than four or five miles a day. Even with ample food from the Minna Bluff Depot, scurvy continues its ravage on all of them.

Conditions are miserable. Their clothing is in tatters, almost worn out as it was second-hand when they started sledging months before. They wear all their clothes now, as they have at night for the entire journey; long underwear, an inner layer of clothing they refer to as their 'pyjama suit', a thick heavy sweater, canvas trousers, a balaclava then a Burberry jacket, and of course gloves, fur mitts and their ski boots, some of which they had concocted over the winter months at Cape Evans. Their mittens and gloves are worn, and absolutely greasy, but they are the least of their troubles. Their main concern is with their outer clothing, their windproof gear, which has become torn in places. Some of them, primarily Joyce and Wild, spend time in the evenings fixing their finneskoe and Burberrys, mitts and socks, whilst lying in their sleeping bags.

During their hours of travel, Mackintosh is now on a sledge most of the time. Hayward is unable to help with the sledge pulling and he now simply walks along with the aid of sticks. So, it is Richards and the two older hardened seamen Joyce and Wild, plus the four dogs, who are hauling the sledges. Spencer-Smith is strapped onto the front sledge and he is still cheerful, but he has hardly moved for weeks.

They are all suffering, but luckily, the legs of Joyce, Richards and Wild are not very stiff. Hayward's knees and ankles have stiffened right up, and it is as much as he can do to get over the ground at anything like a fast pace. The joints of his legs are swollen, and his feet are black, and he can hardly press on them. However, by shutting his eyes and getting his head down he usually finds himself staying close to the others.

When they are outside the tent any fluid in frostbitten blisters freezes hard, and in the evenings, they rub their own – and each other's – faces, hands and feet to revive any parts that appear dead. Hayward is becoming more and more sorrowful: "What a rotten, rotten business this is," he says.

"Vic, you are in a very bad way," says Joyce. "I can see your gums protruding and your legs and feet seem to be giving you great trouble."

"It's all I can do, hang onto the sledge. Pulling any weight in the trace is impossible."

He thinks of his fiancé: "I am now out of the team and I try not to imagine what my Ethel will think of me."

Richards looks at his own legs: "I'm sorry to say that I've also got the dreaded black appearance on the back of my legs, although up to now it has given me little trouble. I don't know whether it's scurvy or not."

Joyce knows the answer to their predicament: "The only possible cure is fresh food."

***

"For God's sake Richie stop or you'll bust your heart," calls Spencer-Smith from the sledge.

Richards finds the pulling more and more taxing, especially when there is a third man on the sledge. Spencer-Smith can see Richards labouring away. Hayward has reached the stage where he can only stumble along in a squatting position under his own steam for a few yards, so he is now invariably on the sledge, with Spencer-Smith and Mackintosh.

On some days there is a mild blizzard blowing but they have to keep moving. At times they can see nothing because of falling snow so Joyce, Richards and Wild simply plod along in the thick blank whiteness. To add to their worries, Mackintosh's condition and demeanour is worsening. One day he falls off sledge three times, and the men ahead hardly hear him shout, because of the heavy wind and snow.

"Sir," says Joyce. "You have to shout as soon as you fall; otherwise you might be left behind."

Mackintosh is disconsolate: "It would be a good job Joyce."

On one evening they come to pitch their tents and find some of the tent poles have fallen off the back sledge. The health of all the men had been deteriorating for some weeks and they were becoming less particular with the packing and lashing of the sledges. Richards is completely exhausted from a day of hauling, but his day is not over. They cannot put up the tent without the poles and Richards wonders what they will do if they have lost them. He stands on the sledge with the binoculars to look back over their track and spots something dark about half a mile away. There is no discussion; Richards goes back to pick them up. When he is back with the poles he mutters to Hayward: "That was the hardest damn journey I ever made."

***

Richards' body jumps. Then his whole-body shakes and shivers as it tries to keep a blood circulation going. It is early morning and the temperature has dropped considerably causing Richards' feet to become extremely cold, and the cold is gradually creeping up his body. His body had started to shiver an hour before and the shivering just does not stop. His body jumps again, and the jumping, the shaking and the shivering continue violently, until it is time for Richards to get up.

The abominable conditions start to affect the mental state of all the men, including the young man from Long Gully. The temperature is below minus 30 degrees Fahrenheit at night, and the nights are closing in earlier and earlier every day. From about four o'clock in the afternoon it is dark, and they have no lights inside the tents.

They are in iced-up sleeping bags and wearing worn clothing, so they have very little sleep. When Richards unfolds his sleeping bag it is like a frozen board, and it is cold ice against his fingers as he separates the flap of the bag. He opens it and then in go his legs followed by the rest of his body. Ice crackles as he edges down in the bag, and then his head meets a shower of snow and ice as he eases the flap over his head and toggles up. The warmth from his body now sets up a thaw, and he turns and shifts position, but it is damp everywhere. The bits of ice on his woollen helmet melt around his face, but somehow, he gets used to it dripping on his face. It is one of his saddest periods of the whole sledging journey.

On one morning, Hayward sums up how he feels, in his typically verbose manner: "It is really unfair to tax anybody's imagination, to the extent required to obtain anything like a fair average idea of the hideous night, the weather and the sleeping bag contrived to make last night for me."

Richards listens, as Hayward goes on.

"I'll only say that I have never had to contend with anything like it and hope I may never have to again."

***

Spencer-Smith's condition is now making Wild very nervous: "Smithy's almost at his last gasp. If we don't quickly make Hut Point it might be fatal."

"I hope we can get in, bar accidents, in four days," says Joyce.

The six men are now less than 40 miles from Hut Point, but even with assistance from a wind for part of the next day they manage only eight miles, putting them around 30 miles from Hut Point by evening.

Like Wild, Joyce is now apprehensive: "Our patients aren't in the best of trim. It seems to me we shall have to leave someone if the wind eases at all."

On the next day it takes four hours to pack up camp. Then they march only one and a half miles in the first two hours, so they lighten their load some more, by dumping one of the sledges and unnecessary gear. Iced up sleeping bags have added to the weight on the sledge. They were about 10 pounds when they were dry but after six months in the field their insides are full of ice. The fur of the bag is on the inside and their breath has condensed on the fur. Each bag now weighs 20 to 25 pounds.

It is the calmest day they have had for weeks; the sun is shining but it is extremely hard going. Hayward and Mackintosh stumble along with sticks, at a very slow pace, their legs bent unceasingly. When Mackintosh collapses, they put him on the back sledge, but this added weight proves too much for the weakening Joyce, Richards and Wild, and the four dogs. They cannot move the sledge, so they camp.

After their meal Joyce and Richards call Wild to their tent to discuss the situation. They feel that Spencer-Smith is close to dying, but if they can get him to Hut Point swiftly, they will save his life, because they are sure seal meat will cure his scurvy.

"It's absolutely necessary that we get fresh food quickly," says Joyce. "Not only for Smithy, for all of us. If we don't do something, we might all perish, even though we are so close to Hut Point."

Richards considers the options: "Well there's only one thing to do. We have to depot the Skipper and proceed in with Smithy, and Vic."

Joyce knows they have to do something: "Unless our speed can be improved the result will be disastrous. The six of us will never get in."

And Wild agrees with Richards' suggestion. "We can leave the Skipper with three weeks food. After we get to Hut Point, and save the padre, we can come back out for Mack."

Joyce, Richards and Wild go over to Mackintosh's tent and tell him what they propose to do, and Mackintosh acquiesces without any complaint. He is only too willing to comply with their wishes. Richards thinks he seems a little dull, as though he doesn't seem to know what is happening, and that he has lost his capacity for clear thought. He is prepared to leave all the decisions to others.

They pitch the conical tent over Mackintosh and set him up with provisions. He is quite comfortable, and he makes no comment other than: "Do anything you like with me Joyce."

***

"How are you feeling Smithy?" asks Richards.

"Not very rather well I am afraid. I have stomach pains, and I think I am bleeding from the bowels."

"You are padre," says Wild. "You have been for some time."

"I can see the blood seeping through your sleeping bag," says Richards.

Joyce, Richards, Hayward, Spencer-Smith and Wild are crammed into a three-man tent. Mackintosh has been left behind. The five men are camped just 20 miles from Hut Point, and it is a terrible night, where the temperature drops down to minus 30; pitch dark and so cold that they all shiver violently the whole night through. Their sleeping bags are now threadbare and full of ice condensed in the fur. None of the five men even doze off for a short time as they spend the night twisting and turning. Sleep in these conditions is impossible.

Smith groans and sings out during the night. To relieve his pains, he is taking opium. At 4 o'clock in the morning he asks Wild the time and when Wild gets up to relive himself Spencer-Smith starts laughing and says: "Have you lost your bearings Tubby?"

Shortly afterwards Spencer-Smith speaks to Richards.

"If your heart's behaving funny Richie, what is the best thing to do, sit up or lie down?"

"I don't know Smithy, but probably best to lie still."

Sometime later Richards looks across at Spencer-Smith, and he sees ice on his eyelashes and beard. He knows he is dead.

"I think he has gone," he yells to the others." I had no idea his death was so near."

From January 29 to this day March 8 when he dies, Spencer-Smith had been on the sledge. Joyce, Richards,

Wild and Hayward consider they did everything they could to make life more comfortable for him and they are upset they had not done more. They know the jolting of the sledge must have been almost unbearable at times, and now, within two days march of comparative safety, his loss seems so tragic after what he had been though.

Hayward cannot believe it: "Last night his thoughts were on how eager he was to get back to the hut. He was quite cheerful about it."

Richards, Joyce and Wild dig a grave and bury him. They have to roll his body in his sleeping bag to the grave dug in the snow as they are too weak to lift it. They put up a small cross made of bamboo flag sticks and build a mound with a cairn over the grave, while Hayward sits against the sledge with his back turned towards the others, refusing to look.

The mood of the four men is understandably sombre as they set off for Hut Point without Spencer-Smith, and with Mackintosh still out on the Barrier on his own. Joyce is out in front for the day's march, with the harness slung over his shoulder, bent forward with the weight of the trace. Now and again he half turns his head to cheer on the dogs and Richards and Wild. Hayward is on the sledge.

They slowly march on, with an unpleasant and unwelcome northerly wind in their faces, and in temperatures below 20 degrees, That night there is little joy in their tent, and Joyce's brief thought on the days sledging matched everyone else's: "I found the going very hard today," he says.

"Even the dogs seem like giving in," says Richards. "They don't have any interest in their work."

Joyce replies: "We've been out much too long, and nothing ahead to cheer us up but a cold, cheerless hut.

In the morning Richards looks through papers they have of Spencer-Smith.

"Here is his diary," he tells the others, as he flicks through the pages. "I can just read it. And here is his last entry before he dies. Something about a Merry Happy Returns of the Day to an 'F'. He mentioned he had a sister Fredrica. He goes on to explain that

Mack would soon be left behind and then he and Vic would remain at the hut while the others would come back with seal-meat for Mack."

Joyce, Wild and Hayward are deep in their own thoughts as Richards goes on.

"And here is a note from Mack, a testimonial to Smithy."

Richards mumbles to himself as he reads it. "Lovely note. Here are Mack's exact words: 'During the winter, which had been passed under the most severe conditions, Mr. Spencer Smith has been the mainstay of the party. His influence over the other members has had a great effect on it being passed, possibly in a manner in which it would not, had he not been with us'."

Hayward cannot take any more: "Richie. Please, just read it to yourself."

"He was a good man in the best sense of the word," says Wild.

"My abiding memory of Smithy is how cheerful he was, all the time, over all those long days where he was lying helpless on the sledge," says Richards. "I was near him as we went along, and we had the opportunity for the occasional word. Towards the latter stages he sometimes sank into a coma and at times I heard him wandering, but he was amazingly optimistic throughout and never at any time lost hope."

Wild, who had spent so much time in close proximity to Spencer-Smith, has very little to add to Richards' comments: "You know, he never once complained."

They guess that scurvy, coupled with Spencer-Smith's previous heart trouble, may have made his heart more liable to an attack of scurvy. They doubt whether the opium he was taking aggravated his condition, as it was taken to send him to sleep.

Richards, Joyce, Wild and Hayward turn in at 10pm, exhausted both mentally and physically. Their efforts to save Spencer-Smith had been in vain.

CHAPTER 16

Spartan conditions at the Discovery hut

Richards, Joyce and Wild, and the four dogs – Oscar, Con, Towser and Gunner – haul the sledge over the last few miles on the Barrier. It is laden with little more than their tent and sleeping bags, and the totally incapacitated Hayward, although he manages to toddle ahead when they have a spell. Their faces are a mass of scabs and postulant sores, and their fingers are black with frostbite.

They reach edge of Ice Barrier where they can see seals and the dogs become very excited. The men struggle to keep the dogs from rushing at them. At a point less than three miles from the *Discovery* hut they find the sea-ice is not frozen, so they cannot walk the last miles directly to the hut, they have to detour a little and are therefore forced to camp for the night on a hill. They haul their gear a little way up the hill – only 150 yards – but every three paces they have to stop and get their breath.

To Wild, it is a most strenuous day. "I've never been more done up," he declares to the others. "Took my sleeping bag up and after every two steps I fell on top of it and had a spell. I rolled it up as I was too weary to carry it. I was in a good mind to open it out and turn in and chance it."

"I'm the same Tubby," says Joyce." I think this is the worst day I've ever spent, and we still have to get Vic to the hut. It's not very entertaining for sleep."

On the next day Joyce, Richards, Wild and Hayward find a way down to the sea-ice and even though the ice is not firm they take the risk and keep going. Hayward manages to get along somehow, but the pain in his legs is excruciating.

When they reach the sea-ice Richards stares at the seals. They are only 100 yards away, by a crack in the ice and Richards suddenly has this inordinate craving for fresh meat. He wants to rush forward and kill a seal and eat the meat raw, but somehow, he holds back this barbaric urge, and within an hour he and Joyce, Wild and Hayward reach the *Discovery* hut.

Mackintosh spends another night alone in his tent, out on the Barrier, about 30 miles from Hut Point.

***

"Hut Point at last!" Wild exclaims.

The *Discovery* hut is just an empty wooden shed, but they are now safe. To these four men the hut represents security, although ice has blocked the door, so they enter through a window, passing Hayward through there as well.

"You know," says Richards. "Without the dogs we would not have got back. They saved our lives."

And Hayward is of the same opinion: "I agree Richie, and I am so grateful we are now safe."

Discovery Hut at Hut Point.

Joyce looks around the hut: "It seems strange. This place has been standing since we built it fifteen years ago. When Scott arrived from his farthest South trek we were here, and we went wild that day. This homecoming is quite different."

But Joyce does not reminisce for long: "First step is to have a cooked meal. I see an old tin of McDoddies dried veges here and then we kill seals for fresh meat."

Richards explains to the others how he was feeling when he first saw the seals: "You know, it's rather extraordinary how my body is now reacting to food. As we crossed the tide crack to go into the hut, there were several seals there and I had this almost overpowering desire to kill one of those seals and to drink its blood."

Hayward cannot believe him: "No Richie!"

"I did. It's extraordinary. It was an almost overpowering desire, like my body was just crying out for it. I felt very close to killing one of them there and then."

Hayward still cannot believe Richards: "You felt you could not wait?" he asks.

"I am sure I would have eaten the meat raw had we not been near the hut, and in a position to cook it immediately."

Richards and Wild kill a seal and they have their first meal of fresh food for months, although they can hardly eat anything at first, because their gums just about cover their teeth.

Hayward has concerns for his health and hopes that his legs will soon improve. He had been working under the same conditions as Joyce and Richards, but he had fallen ill before them. He knows he had not eaten fresh meat as often, because he, like Mackintosh and Spencer-Smith, did not like the taste of seal meat.

At the hut, Richards is sombre, which is unusual for him and it is the first time he can remember being somewhat sorry for himself. He is now safe, but he feels weak and low in spirits; with Mackintosh still out on the Barrier, and because they had just buried Spencer-Smith.

***

They breakfast the next day on porridge, fried seal meat, tinned vegetables and coffee, and it is like a banquet to all of them.

They spend two days drying their gear, mainly their sleeping bags, and killing and cooking seals. Even within these two days, they find the fresh meat improves everyone's health. So, they plan to depart on the following day, taking sufficient cooked seal meat for them and the dogs for the journey out to Mackintosh, and back. Hayward will stay in the hut, and he is extremely disappointed at being unable to travel, so he could be involved in the rescue of Mackintosh.

"How I wish I was fit and able go out again. But I absolutely cannot bend my knees straight and to walk is agonizing."

Joyce points at the supply of cooked seal meat on the stove top: "You have all you need at hand. I think you can manage well enough until our return."

Joyce, Richards, Wild and the four dogs set off south, and Hayward mutters to himself: "So now I start my arbitrary bachelordom for a week."

The three men make excellent progress, ten miles on the first day, and in their tent that evening Joyce surveys his two companions.

"We are a wild looking party. The most ragged lot one could meet in a day's march. Our faces are as black as niggers, a sort of crowd one would run away from."

After a second excellent day's travel, Joyce is very pleased: "We are going along at a rattling good rate; in spite of our swollen limbs. We have done about fifteen miles."

On the third day out they see Mackintosh's tent, a few hours after they had passed Spencer-Smith's grave. On arrival they find Mackintosh outside the tent, much to their joy as they expected him to be down. His rotting clothes hang from his frail body, and his teeth are now sunken well into his gums which are black and badly swollen. His remaining eye is monstrously bloated. He tells them that he has managed to hobble around a little each day.

They break the news of Smith's death and Mackintosh appears to take it well. Richards thinks he looks a little dazed, as though the news did not make a big impression on him. And Richards is surprised that Mackintosh does not even say something like bad luck, but he puts this down to his lonely vigil on the Barrier. However, Mackintosh does know his life has been saved: "I cannot thank you all enough. When I saw you coming, I thought that this is the best time of my life."

"How are you Sir?" asks Wild the Petty Officer, ever maintaining his respect for Navy rank.

"I think I am all right."

"We hope to get you to the hut in three days and then fresh food will improve you."

They set off but find that Mackintosh can only shuffle along with aid of two sticks, so they put him on the sledge. They only travel a mile that day before camping, and as Joyce sets up the cooker inside the tent, he takes some pride in announcing the menu for his officer: "A banquet coming up for you tonight Sir. Seal meat, vegetables and black current jam. It will be the feed of your life."

"I have had the most peculiar dreams Joyce, while out there on my own. I slept in a semi-conscious state where I found myself talking to imaginary people in the tent."

They wake at five the next morning and by eight they are underway, with Mackintosh feeling better already. They pass Spencer-Smith's grave, make close to 20 miles for the day, and after a very cold night of minus 30 degrees, they reach the *Discovery* hut the next evening.

Wild is ecstatic: "Hut Point again. Hooray!"

They have exceeded their utmost expectation, covering about 80 miles in three days, with Mackintosh on the sledge on the returning journey. At the hut they find Hayward about the same, but he and all the others are now in the best of spirits. The dogs have lost their lassitude and are quite frisky, except Oscar who is suffering from overfeeding.

"Plenty of exercise and fresh food ought to do miracles," says Joyce. "My ankles and knees are badly swollen as are my gums. How is everyone else feeling?"

Hayward is the first to speak: "My lips and gums are black and so swollen I cannot even see my teeth, and I cannot straighten my knees at all. They are not swollen and only slightly black, but I walk like a bent up old man. Even my elbows are stiff and sore."

"I can see the pupils of your eyes are enlarged Vic," says Wild. "My right leg behind the knee is black and slightly swollen. Like you my gums are very swollen."

For some reason – possibly his younger age and his good health – Richards is better off than Joyce and Wild, and certainly Hayward. He has some discoloration behind his knees, and his gums are slightly swollen, that's all.

Joyce examines Mackintosh and finds he is blue from his right hip bone down to his knee. He is swollen from the knee to the ankle and the ankle is blown up way out of proportion. His gums are swollen but not particularly black, and the white of his eye is distended.

Joyce is confident that with fresh meat and exercise they will all quickly recover. He is thankful their long journey is now over: "We have been out 160 days, and done a distance of over 1500 miles, a good record. I think the irony of fate was poor Smith going under a day before we got in. I think we shall all soon be well."

Richards is very proud of their work: 'We have the satisfaction of knowing that we have completed our task."

"That's right Richie," says Joyce. "Shacks will have had sufficient food over the latter part of his journey."

Mackintosh shakes hands with Joyce, Richards, Wild and Hayward. He is almost overcome with emotion.

"Thank you for saving my life. My wife and children will bless you."

Inside the Discovery Hut.

Richards feels like a troglodyte, an ancient person living in a cave, because conditions at the *Discovery* hut are primitive, very primitive. The hut is only a shell with one layer of wooden boards between them and the bitterly Antarctic winter outside. The hut was built for 45 people, but it is two thirds full of snow and ice and there are no tables, chairs or bunks. The five men live in one small area, partially partitioned off with some empty cases and tarpaulins. They live in their clothes, lying down inside their sleeping bags, because it is too cold if they sit up in the bag. There is a fireplace, which is their stove, in the centre of the partitioned off area and this is made up of nothing more than a sheet of iron over some bricks. They eat and sleep around the stove, on planks resting on old provision boxes.

Their sole heating comes from burning seal blubber chunks, and as soon as they put any blubber into the stove the hut fills up with smoke. Their clothes soon become saturated with blubber and seal blood, and even though they do not notice the smell, they know they are all in a filthy condition. They never take their off their clothes or wash as they have no facilities for heating a large quantity of water, let alone any soap. They have no lighting; all they have is an improvised blubber lamp, made out of a bit of string in some blubber oil in an old tin, and this tiny blubber lamp gives out copious amounts of fumes and very little light.

Typically, matter-of-fact Wild tells everyone: "We shall settle down here now for a couple of months."

It is mid-March, but it will be June or July before they can expect the open water between Hut Point and Cape Evans to freeze over. Only then can they walk the 13 miles safely over the sea-ice to the well-appointed Cape Evans hut, where they assume Cope, Stevens, Gaze and Jack are waiting for them. Soon it will be dark for the whole 24 hours which means they are restricted to periods of full moon to make the journey across, even if the sea freezes firmly. Consequently, they resign themselves to a rather protracted stay. Although it is possible to go around the land to Cape Evans, they don't even contemplate taking that route, as they have no equipment, and they would need daylight to make the trip anyway.

They set up a routine, based around set times for meals; a morning meal at seven o'clock, lunch at two, dinner at seven in the evening and they retire at about half past nine. Meals somehow are the principal event of the day. Before one is prepared the five men discuss – quite thoroughly – how it is to be prepared, as one person may like the seal meat fried, another may like it made into a stew. Then they criticise any suggested methods of cooking, where a friendly argument may crop up.

Joyce, Richards and Wild are soon able to go about their daily tasks with reasonable efficiency, and they manage to chip away all the ice blocking the door to the hut. However, Mackintosh has some internal haemorrhaging and neither he nor Hayward can straighten their legs more than a little past a right angle. At first everyone's teeth are barely visible owing to the gums coming down over them and it is impossible to eat a biscuit without first soaking it in tea first.

There is a small supply of biscuits in the hut, which Joyce thinks have been there for 16 years, but there is no tobacco.

"Oh, for a pipe of tobacco," he wails.

The biscuits, the few tins of vegetables and 'luxury' items like coffee and flour and jam in the hut do not last more than a day or two, and from then on virtually their sole food is seal meat. They eat it morning, noon and night, day after day, but they are confident they will soon recover from scurvy, on this diet. And they do. Richards is astounded at how quickly Mackintosh and Hayward recover. Seal meat proves remarkably effective in curing their scurvy. The size of all their meals is truly prodigious, as their bodies seem to demand an inordinate amount of meat and they see each other gaining strength from day to day. Fortunately, in March, seals are plentiful with many lazing about on the sea-ice around Hut Point.

In the hut one afternoon Joyce stands with Hayward around the stove.

"Richards and Wild are still doing good work sealing Vic. They have brought in 10 since we have been back."

"The dogs are out sealing too, with them."

"Yes, although a peculiar thing. They will not touch the flesh while you are killing but wait until the meat is frozen before eating it."

However, after a month, the seal population around the hut dwindles and seal hunting becomes much more difficult. On some days the men searching for seals walk for over ten miles in the gloomy darkness without seeing one. Richards and Wild kill two penguins one day, and as an indication of their cave man type of existence, Wild says to the others: "Richy and I got two more Emperors today. We will skin them and try and dress the skins for clothes."

The five men live in barbaric type conditions, but they are safe, and they live together quite harmoniously. Everyone is in good spirits and Mackintosh and Hayward's health continues to improve, as does their demeanour. Hayward says to the others one evening: "Skipper and I did the goose step for an hour or so by way of exercise."

Richards, Joyce and Wild have returned to the Barrier and rescued Mackintosh. There are five men at the rudimentary *Discovery* hut, only 13 miles from the comparatively luxurious Cape Evans hut.

CHAPTER 17

Impatience

"I'm thinking of this time next year," says Mackintosh to Hayward. "Home Sweet Home, all that life's worth living and hoping for."

He tells Hayward of his thoughts, of returning to England to see his family, and how he is looking forward to getting away from the *Discovery* hut as soon as possible.

"What a joy it will be to get back to the hut at Cape Evans, or even better my cabin on the *Aurora,* and have that wash and put on clean clothes once again."

Richards, Joyce and Wild accept they will be living at the *Discovery* hut for some months, until it is safe to walk to the hut at Cape Evans. However, the attitude of Mackintosh and Hayward is quite different. Within a few weeks conditions in the hut start to become unbearable for both men, particularly Mackintosh.

Inside the hut they are confined to the partitioned off area where they live and it is always full of smoke, from the stove burning blubber. The only concession to bettering their lifestyle is an occasional cutting of hair and trimming of the beard. Their clothes are begrimed with blubber and their faces black with soot, and Mackintosh cannot get used to the grime and dirt. Blubber which has overflowed from the stove is lying everywhere on the floor, so he and the others are always walking in it. When anyone has to re-stoke the stove, with a new piece of blubber, that person has to get down on his knees at the stove, where his hands and legs become smothered in the old blubber that is on the floor. This person places a piece of new blubber in the opening, applies a match to it and after gentle manipulation – which requires much patience – he gets it burning. Mackintosh can hardly bear tasks like this and he feels he is leading the life of an uncivilised person.

He sits with Hayward, huddled up alongside of the stove.

"Here we are, sitting over this stove in a bent-up position like Indians over a fire. But the dirt, it's too terrible. Everything we touch is blubber which, added with the smoke is as a dirty a mixture for blackening one as could be manufactured. The worst of this is that it soaks into one's clothes."

"What will it be like in another month Skipper, if we should be here?"

Mackintosh is even concerned with their appearance: "What a crowd of utter tramps we look; long matted hair, un-cropped straggling beards, grease all over ourselves, and our clothes."

"Dirtiness personified."

"Oh! This filth. When will we be released?"

An extended blizzard that lasts for two weeks in April produces a gigantic snow drift by the door, and this keeps Richards and Wild constantly busy with a shovel. With a blizzard raging the five men can do little but curl up in their sleeping bags. The slow burning blubber stove provides little heat and the temperature inside the hut drops to 20 below zero. Water in a pot by the stove is frozen.

Mackintosh tells Richards of a book called *Five John Street,* a story about a well-to-do man who learns what it is like to live on half-a-crown a day in the slums of the West End of London. Mackintosh compares his predicament to the author of the book.

"Richards, the inhabitants there were clean in respect to us. Who on earth could be filthier than us? Our clothes are deplorable; Hayward is walking about on his uppers."

In the gloomy almost lightless hut, the five men do the best they can to entertain themselves, with debates and sing-alongs. At one time Hayward argues with Mackintosh and Joyce on the respective merits of the conditions in Canada as compared to those in the Antarctic. Hayward states that the blizzards in Canada are more severe than in the Antarctic and Canadian cowboys are able to get out in any weather. Richards and Wild lie in their bags enjoying the argument.

There is a small quantity of reading matter left there by previous occupants, and some books are read over and over, especially *Lorna Doone.* Joyce is unable to read on account of snow-blindness, so Richards and Wild read to him now and again, not that reading is easy, with the light provided by a flickering wick from a blubber lamp.

In mid-April, Richards notices the sun at midday is staying very low in the sky. He knows it will disappear altogether within the next few days, and not return for four months, but he is happy with his lot. He is prepared to wait at the *Discovery* hut, optimistic that he and the other four men, with their four dogs, will walk to Cape Evans in a couple of months when the sea-ice is thick, and be rescued in the next summer.

When no one is talking, Richards listens to the grinding and crunching of sea-ice to the north of the hut.

Makeshift lantern at Discovery Hut.

***

Mackintosh and Hayward are out walking.

"I try to get out as much as possible Victor. Breathing all that carbon in the hut can't be good for one."

"A little fresh air acts as an antidote Skipper."

Mackintosh points to the north, towards Cape Evans.

"Yesterday I saw killer whales there, sporting about and breaking up the sea-ice. The ice looked about eight inches thick and these whales simply made great lanes through it with the utmost ease."

"I would not like to be on that ice," says Hayward, "and see ones ground broken up under ones feet."

Towards the end of April and in early May, Mackintosh and Hayward have been taking walks in the twilight, when the weather is fair, to check the condition of the sea-ice. There is a short period of twilight for about five hours on either side of noon, in clear weather. They are disappointed when the wind blows the ice to sea, because this postpones their chances of reaching Cape Evans.

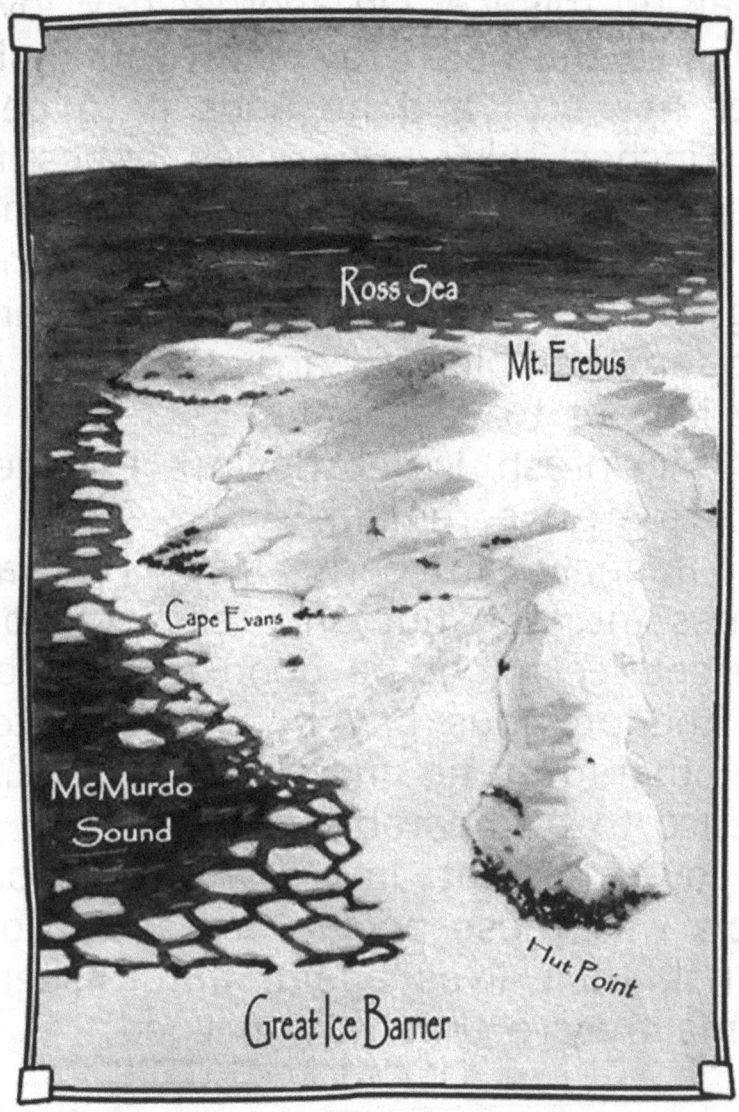

McMurdo Sound showing the 13 miles between Hut Point and Cape Evans.

On one day they check the ice thickness and find it to be about two inches thick, but then another blizzard sets in and the strong wind starts to break up this ice. On another day Joyce walks to the north for about four miles over new ice, and he finds it to be a few inches thick. He raises hopes for everyone, particularly Mackintosh, when he says that in about two days, they might be able to walk to Cape Evans. But, another blizzard arrives, taking all the ice out to sea again.

Mackintosh is let down: "Prisoners once more we remain."

Suddenly, in early May, Hayward comes into the hut and tells everyone the sea-ice might be good to walk on. On the previous day he had also told the others that he and Mackintosh found the ice to be bearable.

Joyce is not impressed: "I don't know why these people are so anxious to risk their lives again, but it seems to me they're that way inclined."

***

On the eighth of May Mackintosh makes a sudden and unexpected announcement: "Hayward and I are going to Cape Evans today."

Joyce frowns. He stands up and goes outside to look at the weather, and it is fine and calm at Hut Point. It is the middle of the day with some twilight, so he looks southward towards the Minna Bluff landmark, which they use as an indicator of the weather ahead. If the weather is going to remain fine, they can see the bluff from Hut Point, but if the bluff is obscured, they know bad weather is coming. Joyce cannot see the bluff, so he goes back inside.

"Now look Sir, you may call me old cautious, but I wouldn't go to Cape Evans today for all the tea in China. The Bluff has a covering over it, and it looks very dark to the south."

Richards glances at Hayward, who seems to have an uncertain look on his face after hearing these words of Joyce.

Joyce goes on: "Although Cape Evans is only three and a half hours journey without a sledge, it would be hell to be caught in a blizzard on thin sea-ice. I think we will have a blizzard within two hours, and it would be very foolish to attempt it."

"Oh, nonsense Joyce, we'll be alright," says Mackintosh.

Richards is very surprised by Mackintosh's decision. He and Hayward are now walking freely but they have not walked more than a mile or two at one time.

"Mack, do you have the strength to walk the 13 miles to Cape Evans?" asks Richards.

"We'll travel light."

"I don't think it's the day for it," says Joyce.

"I'm going," replies Mackintosh.

Although Joyce, Richards and Wild are not in favour there is not much they can do. Mackintosh is still in charge, and short of forcibly restraining him they can only urge him not to go. Richards sees that Hayward still appears a little dubious.

***

Mackintosh and Hayward leave, carrying nothing more than a bag of cold seal meat and some personal diaries and papers. They take no extra gear at all. They are just walking across. To Joyce, Richards and Wild it is madness and they do not even consider joining them. In fact, if

Mackintosh had ordered them to join him, they would have told him to go to hell.

Joyce, Richards and Wild stand on the top of a small hill next to the *Discovery* hut and watch Mackintosh and Hayward head north over the sea-ice. There is only a dull light in the middle of the day, and it is not long before they can only see their two companions rather dimly. They look almost pygmy-like as they grow fainter and fainter.

The three men say nothing until Mackintosh and Hayward are out of sight, but Richards then breaks the silence, to reveal how unhappy he is with Mackintosh's decision: "We've worked our guts out to get them to the safety of Hut Point."

Joyce has similar thoughts to Richards: "I did not want anyone to risk going to Cape Evans before the sea-ice was firm."

"I'm feeling bitter about the whole bloody thing Joycey. It's a needless risk."

And Wild feels much the same way: "If they get lost, I'll be sorry we humped them back here over the Barrier, but let's hope they get there alright."

The three men turn back and walk down to the hut. Sure enough, in little more than an hour, the wind begins to rise and before long the blizzard Joyce had predicted arrives. Joyce, Richards and Wild lie in their sleeping bags in the hut, and they can think of nothing else but Mackintosh and Hayward.

"It is impossible to exist in these conditions with no equipment," says Joyce.

***

Two sets of footprints are clearly visible, raised up in on ice flowers; ice crystals that look like small flowers, which develop on freshly formed sea-ice. Joyce, Richards and Wild follow the footprints for over a mile and then one of the sets of footprints turns towards the shore. Suddenly, both sets of footprints end abruptly and in the dim light Richards notices a difference in the look of the ice. He pushes a stick in the ice, and it goes straight through.

"That where the ice went out, I think," he indicates to Joyce and Wild.

The three men look ahead, and in the gloom, they see a wide stretch of open water, very lightly covered with ice, as far as their eyes can see.

"That ice is only one night's freezing," says Joyce.

Richards stares ahead. "It seems clear to me. The part of the ice over which Mack and Vic have travelled has gone out to sea."

It is May 10, two days after Mackintosh and Hayward had left. Joyce, Richards and Wild are walking over the sea-ice to the north, tracing Mackintosh and Hayward's footsteps on the soft slushy ice.

Joyce fears the worst: "The blizzard has taken the ice out. There will be open water to the north. Whether they got there or no they deserved to be badly frostbitten or lose their lives. After dragging them back from death they seem to think they can court it again."

"Well such is life, and what fools we got to put up with," adds Wild.

Wild's next words create a horrific picture in Richards' mind.

"Perhaps they've gone out on a flow."

Joyce, Richards and Wild say nothing more. They turn around and head back to the *Discovery* hut. That evening they say very little to each other, with the realisation that Mackintosh and Hayward have probably just thrown away their lives.

After their dinner meal they lie in their sleeping bags immersed in their own thoughts for a while, but then Joyce opens up a conversation that lasts for some time: "You know, we have suffered greatly in saving their lives, and now they have risked everything on some sort of whim."

For Richards in particular, all the reservations about Mackintosh's quality as a leader resurface: "One thing I can say is that Mackintosh was a quite unsuitable choice as a leader. The man had no judgment or qualities of leadership to fit him for the job."

"Plucky as they come Richie," says Wild.

But Richards struggles to give Mackintosh any credit: "I know, but the job of our depot laying on the

Beardmore and every degree back from there for six men should have been simple enough."

Joyce continues the criticism of Mackintosh: "I think he could have lost the lives of his own party on the Barrier; Tubby here, Smithy and himself. He would have, if it wasn't for us seeing the position pretty clearly and insisting on going on with him to place the final depot at the Beardmore."

"They have only just recovered from their scurvy," says Richards. "And they could only just walk now without any trouble."

It was "I feel sorry for Vic," says Wild. "He just went with the Skipper without saying anything."

Richards agrees. "Yes. He looked very dubious when Joycey said it was a big risk. But Vic never ever said much. His thoughts were like a sealed book."

Richards, Joyce and Wild cannot stop thinking and talking about Mackintosh, and Hayward. Their conversation pauses for a while, then Richards asks the question that all of them had been mulling over privately.

"Why did he risk his life?" asks Richards.

"He often talked about a way to make the journey," says Wild, "by simply walking back on his own, or with one companion and taking nothing with them."

Joyce's irritation with Mackintosh is clear: "No-one to blame but himself. He's been down here before and he knew of the fragility of the weather."

"That's right," adds Wild. "I remember him saying once that it could change from Paradise to Hades in a few hours."

Richards has his own ideas on why Mackintosh wanted to get away from the *Discovery* hut: "Well, in my opinion, his desire to risk a crossing to Cape Evans was based on his dislike of the primitive conditions here."

Wild and Joyce listen as Richards goes on.

"Mack was quite fond of comfort and there is none whatever in this hut. It is just horrific. To him, Cape Evans is a palace, with lighting, hot water for a bath, bunks to sleep in and blankets. I reckon he said to himself, 'I could get across to Cape Evans; the Sound seems to be frozen over all the way'".

Wild has some sympathy for Mackintosh: "As leader he may have also been anxious to find out whether Cope and the others at Cape Evans were safe."

But Richards disagrees: "I am more inclined to believe that Mack could not put up with the conditions here. I think that outweighed everything else on his mind. He dreaded staying here any longer than was absolutely necessary and he hated the putrid conditions, how his face was black with soot and how everything he touched was stinking of blubber. He hated the smoke-filled hut. He hated living a life of what he called primitive people."

CHAPTER 18

The return of the Aurora, with Shackleton on board

Oscar, Gunner, Towser and Con pull hard on their traces as they close in on the hut at Cape Evans. The four dogs then start to bark, sensing or hearing the presence of other dogs at the hut.

Inside the hut, Cope, Stevens, Jack and Gaze are surprised when their dogs, the bitch Nell and her pups, start to bark. Then they hear other dogs, and men's voices. They scramble out of the hut to see three men and four dogs hauling a sledge towards them.

Joyce shouts at them: "Are Mackintosh and Hayward here?"

Cope is stunned. "No," he calls back. "They headed this way three months ago."

It is mid-July and Joyce, Richards and Wild have made the crossing to Cape Evans from Hut Point. Cope,

Stevens, Jack and Gaze are shocked to hear that Mackintosh and Hayward had attempted to cross earlier, but like Joyce, Richards and Wild they are absolutely convinced that Mackintosh and Hayward are lost and dead.

Cope, who had been sledging with Richards in the first season, is pleased to see the young Australian.

"Hello Richy."

"How are you Copey?" replies Richards.

"I'm not good. I think I've got appendicitis. I'm shitting nanny goats turds."

Richards, Joyce and Wild soon have a bath, their first for 300 days, and then a meal that they relish; something other than the seal meat they had been eating for months. It is a sea-leopard that had been killed and Joyce cooks it for himself, Richards and Wild.

"Wait 'til you try these flippers Richie," says Joyce. "Fried, they are wonderful, and the brains."

"Try its tongue Rich, it's delicious," Cope adds.

For the last half of 1916, Joyce, Richards and Wild, with Cope, Stevens,

Jack and Gaze, live at Cape Evans in reasonable comfort. As well as seal meat, penguin meat and penguin eggs they have stores that Scott had left (tinned vegetables, jams, sugar, flour and biscuits) and beds to sleep on. They have an insulated hut with lighting and a few books and papers to read, although they rarely wash or shave, and sleep in their clothes inside their sleeping bags, under Jaeger blankets.

In August, Richards scribbles a message on the wall next to his bunk, (with an incorrect spelling of Spencer-Smith's name).[1]

R.W. Richards, August 14 1916
Losses to date, Hayward, Mack, Smyth, ship?

Richards' message on the wall of the Cape Evans hut.

There is a sad day when Con, the Samoyed lead dog, is attacked by the other three dogs and killed. Richards, Joyce and Wild are dispirited by the loss. For Richards, Con was a dog with special characteristics, and he was Wild's favourite.

There was the barest chance they might find the bodies of Mackintosh and

Hayward so after the return of the sun – in mid-August – searches are carried out, but without success.

***

"Richie's collapsed," yells Joyce.

Suddenly, one day in December and without warning, Richards falls over outside the Cape Evans hut.

Wild rushes forward.

"What's happened Joycey?"

"I don't know. Richie just threw up his arms, cried out and fainted."

Wild calls for help: "Cope. We need you."

Joyce, Wild and Cope, the only man with some medical knowledge, carry Richards into the hut and put him on a bunk.

Wild is very worried: "Cope, see what you can do. I think the long journey has strained his heart."

Joyce is beside himself. "He was my constant companion for ten months. A better pal never existed, through all our troubles."

After examining Richards, Cope offers some words of encouragement: "I think he'll be alright."

"I hope so," replies Joyce." I feel a broken man."

For Richards, Mackintosh and Hayward's deaths were tragic. It was the final fatal tragedy of the expedition and the heartbreak and the strain were too much for the young man.

Cope, who had been acting strangely for some time, staying in his bunk all day and not eating anything but then raiding the larder in the middle of the night, starts nursing the sick Richards. He shifts Richards from his ordinary bunk into Scott's old bunk and brings Richards his food every day.

"You are nursing me like my mother," Richards tells him.

Richards stays in bed at the Cape Evans hut for a month, but slowly recovers and then manages to walk around with the aid of a stick.

All the seven men can do is wait for January and February and see what comes in the way of relief, but they are not optimistic. They think the *Aurora* has been lost. At times they talk about what they will do if a relief ship does not come, particularly as they knew the war was on. However, Wild is always optimistic. "The war will be over by now. A ship will come."

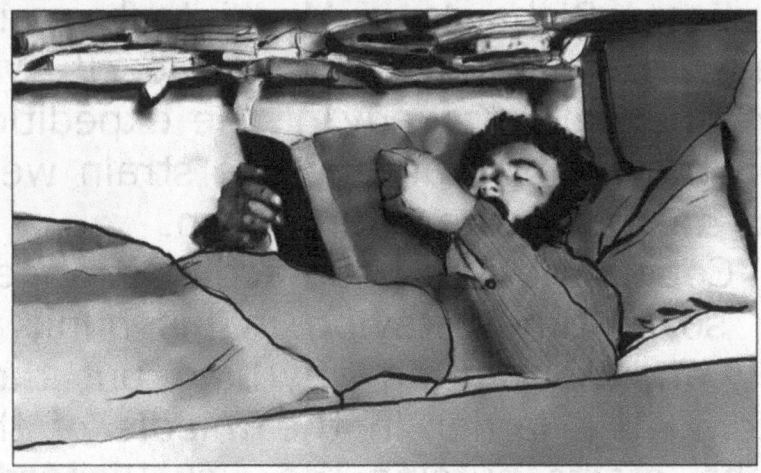

Sketch of Richards recuperating at Cape Evans.

But Joyce has doubts: "The war may not be over."

Richards listens as the others talk and he is also pessimistic: "Either way, whether the war is over or not, we are very small potatoes, and quite negligible I fear."

***

While he is convalescing Richards' job after breakfast is to go outside the hut and look for seals. On January 10, 1917 he looks seaward and notices some sort of shape about seven miles out to sea which at first, he thinks may be an iceberg. Then he sees a plume of smoke and realises a ship is there, so he races back to the hut.

"The ship's here," he yells to the others inside the hut. "The bloody ship."

No-one believes him. Wild shouts: "Don't be a bloody fool."

However, Stevens does come outside to look, and he calls out: "By jove, there is something there."

The others rush outside too, and once they realise a ship is actually there, they all scurry around to load up the sledges with items that have to be taken back. They then set off to travel across seven miles of sea-ice to the ship.

It starts to sink in for Richards that a relief ship is truly there. Tears are in his eyes as he realises his long-time of waiting is over at last. No more hunting for seals, no more blizzards and frostbitten feet and hands. It is too good to be true and he is almost overcome.

After a couple of hours walking, they see three tiny dots, which turn out to be three men, coming across the ice from the ship, and Joyce recognises one as Shackleton. The *Aurora,* with Shackleton on board, has arrived at McMurdo Sound to rescue them.

It is Richards' first meeting with Shackleton, who shakes hands with everyone. He then asks Joyce: "How many men have been lost?"

Joyce replies three, so Shackleton and his two companions lie down the ice, which is a signal back to the ship indicating the number of lives lost.

Joyce is very surprised to see Shackleton, under these circumstances.

"What happened to your party Boss?"

"The *Endurance* was lost, and the party is back home."

When Richards hears of the loss of the *Endurance,* before it even landed Shackleton, it does not even register on him that the labour and suffering of he, Joyce and Wild have been for nothing. He speaks quietly to Joyce: "You know Joycey. I don't look on our struggle as being futile. It was something that the human spirit accomplished."

The *Aurora* is under command of Captain John King Davis. He is astonished at what a profound effect such a long period of isolation has had on the seven men he has rescued: Joyce, Richards, Wild, Cope, Stevens, Jack and Gaze. To Davis they are about the wildest looking gang of men he has ever seen. Their smoke-bleared eyes squint out at him from grey haggard faces, with beards and uncut matted hair impregnated with soot and grease. He notices their eyes have a strained and harassed look, which he is not surprised with, given what they had endured. They had lost their ship eighteen months before, there was the toll of two seasons sledging, the loss of three companions, a lack of suitable clothing and proper food and the almost incessant storms and blizzards. To Davis what would have been worst of all were the weary months waiting for a rescue that might be delayed for another year. All these factors combined to change the men into individuals unlike any he had ever met. The mark of their physical and mental hardships went far deeper than their appearance. He writes in his log: 'Their speech is jerky, semi-hysterical and at times almost unintelligible'.

A cross is erected on the hill behind Cape Evans, in memory of Mackintosh, Hayward and Spencer-Smith, and on January 17 Richards and the others leave McMurdo Sound on the *Aurora*.

On board, Shackleton presents Richards (and Joyce) with a prismatic compass, and on the back of Richards' he engraves an inscription, using his diamond ring.

To R.W. Richards

From E.H. Shackleton.

For Richards the compass becomes his greatest keepsake from his days in the Antarctic. It has emotional associations for him, particularly in the difficult six days of the blizzard in February 1916 when they searched for the Bluff Depot and then turned south again to try and locate Mackintosh, Spencer-Smith and Wild. Richards knew their lives depended on it.

A member of *Aurora's* crew asks Richards what aspect of his adventure registers most in his mind. For Richards there was one incident that stood out more than any other.

"It was finding the tent, a little speck in the white wilderness;

It reaches deeper into me than anything else."

Cross erected at Cape Evans for Mackintosh, Hayward, and Spencer-Smith.

***

[1]   The message is still faintly visible after more than 100 years.

Epilogue on Mackintosh and Hayward

No trace of Mackintosh and Hayward has ever been found.

However, we have a description of what most certainly happened to them, and poignantly it is provided by Mackintosh himself.[2]

On the *Nimrod* expedition Mackintosh had been sent back to New Zealand after the accident where a boat hook hit his right eye. He returns to McMurdo Sound a year later, in January 1909. Due to pack ice the ship is stopped 25 miles away from the hut where the shore party is based so Mackintosh and three sailors leave the ship to take the mail to the hut. They are pulling a sledge as they need to carry a large postage bag, plus their tent, sleeping bags, cooking equipment and food. After four hours of hauling one of the sailors begins to show signs of fatigue so he and another sailor return to the ship, while Mackintosh and the remaining sailor, McGillan, push on.

That night they camp on the sea-ice but the next morning they come across open water, so they start back for the ship. However, they soon come across more open water. We have Mackintosh's own words from his diary at that time which provide a graphic description of their predicament, and how close they come to losing their lives when caught on a floating sheet of ice:

The first intimation that everything was not well was the sight of a whale sprouting. I thought it was just a Killer coming up as they often do to breathe in a seal hole, so no further notice was taken and on we trudged.

Ten minutes later to my horror I saw water ahead and the ice moving rapidly. It seemed impossible and to make quite sure I had a good look from an elevated position. There was no room left for doubt for the immense ice sheet had formed into flows by the numerous cracks developing into lanes of open water.

The cold knowledge that we were very much adrift was anything but cheering. We thought we were then about two and a half miles from shore, but it must have been four in the least.

Mackintosh, and his companion McGillan, are now in a precarious situation, on sea-ice that is breaking up and facing the possibility of being carried out to sea. Mackintosh continues:

There was water to the southward, water to the northward and we were between the two and would before long be floating out to sea! So, a bee line was made for the nearest shore. Across floes, hummocks, and deep snow we dragged our sledge, both realising the necessity of a speedy arrival at the nearest land.

The two men struggle to pull their sledge over the ice floes, towards the shore.

At places we had to lift the sledge bodily over the rough ice face.

In spite of the cold weather we were sweating freely the extra work that now came upon us was back

> breaking. I cannot express the keen and ready way in which McGillan stood by me, and the way in which he showed his willingness to assist me in every way.

Now the situation has become dire, with the size of the ice floes diminishing. Through Mackintosh's words we can imagine what must have been going through his mind at this critical time:

> Our arrival at the first point of land filled us with horror and disgust as we found an impassable lane of water stopping our progress! With all out strength we dragged on to the next point which appeared to be safe.
>
> How we pulled: the floes were getting square in shape and smaller. At about every 200 yards we had to drag our sledge to the edge of a floe and then jump on to the next one ourselves, and with a big effort pull it to safety.
>
> For an hour this kind of work lasted, our hands were cut and bleeding, our clothes wet through to the waist which of course froze

as stiff as boards on us, for we had, when crossing from floe to floe, frequently fallen and slipped on the edge.

Finally, they come close to a glacier that allows them to jump onto solid ground:

Luck however was with us at last, and it cheered me when my companion told me that he had always had good luck. At 2.30pm we were near to the land and came to a piece of detached glacier that formed a bridge apparently to the shore. The flow that we were on was moving rapidly, so we had to make a great effort and drag our sledge over the six feet breach.

Our luck was in and we pulled the sledge a little way up the face of the ice and unpacked it. We were on terra firma! But none too soon for fifteen minutes later there was open water where we had gained the land!

It is not difficult to imagine that Mackintosh and Hayward were in much the same predicament in 1916. However then, tragically, there was no detached glacier that formed a bridge the shore.

There is little doubt that Mackintosh and Hayward were taken out to sea on an ice floe.

Sketch of Mackintosh and Hayward on an ice flow.

***

[2] *Shackleton's lieutenant: the Nimrod diary of A.L.A. Mackintosh,* British Antarctic Expedition, 1907-09.

Richards the unsung hero

Richards is the only Australian to be awarded the Albert Medal – Britain's premier decoration for civilian acts of gallantry – for saving life in the Antarctic.

However, unlike Mawson, Richards' feats during the 'Heroic Age of the Antarctic' are relatively unknown. His acts of bravery and self-sacrifice are not celebrated or recognized. He is an unsung hero.

Richards joined Shackleton's support team when it arrived in Australia, but it was not expected that he would play a major role in the depot laying work. Due to unforeseen circumstances, Richards became more than an integral member of this support contingent; he took over a leadership role. Despite his comparative youth, and inexperience in polar conditions, Richards adapted and survived, unlike some of his companions. He demonstrated what humans can do to stay alive, against near-impossible odds.

Despite incredible obstacles, losing their support ship and most of their dogs, Richards and the others were able to accomplish their designated task; of laying the depots for Shackleton's planned crossing.

Then, with his English colleagues, he undertook a 300 plus mile return trek to base camp with an incapacitated man strapped on a sledge. He and the others had no one to turn to if insurmountable difficulties arose. They were completely alone.

A blizzard halted their progress when only 80 miles from safety. They were in a situation remarkably like that of Scott's fateful final days but Richards (with Joyce and Hayward) fought off the lethargy brought on by scurvy and made a move in the continuing blizzard.

These three men then performed one of the most selfless acts in the history of exploration when they went on a six-day journey through an unrelenting blizzard to a depot to bring back food to their starving companions. The bravery and courage displayed by Richards and his two companions was the difference between life and death.

It was Richards' decision to take bearings of the back cairns on their way south, so they had a route to follow to the depot. As well as having bearings to follow, it was Richards' work in steering Joyce that saved all their lives.

The young man Richards also shouldered a leadership role when Mackintosh weakened, and when vital decisions had to be made; to leave Mackintosh, Spencer-Smith and Wild behind at one time, and then Mackintosh at a later stage.

Then, finally, with Joyce and Wild, Richards displayed an incredible will to live as the three of them dragged a sledge with the incapacitated Hayward to reach the safety of Hut Point, and then return to rescue Mackintosh.

When one learns of the achievements of Richards in the Antarctic, the question arises: why does Richards not feature alongside Douglas Mawson when eulogising Australia's participation in the 'Heroic Age' in the Antarctic?

For Shackleton, the efforts of Richards and the others of his Ross Sea party constituted:

> *...the most remarkable story of human endeavour that has ever been revealed. Mackintosh and Hayward owed their lives on that journey to the unremitting care and strenuous endeavours of Joyce, Wild, and Richards, who, also scurvy-stricken but fitter than their comrades, dragged them through the deep snow and blizzards on the sledges.*[3]

Australian Prime Minister Bob Hawke wrote about Richards in 1984:

> *Your incredible journey of almost 2000 miles across the Antarctic Wastelands – involving some nine months in the field with makeshift equipment – and your adherence to duty in the face of enormous difficulty, suffering from scurvy, and the death of comrades, will be an inspiration to your countrymen of the future as it is to us today.*

There are numerous books on Mawson, but not on Richards and 'Historians and geographers have noted that Australian Antarctic popular history has been written and consumed through a frame of heroic masculinity centred on Mawson'.[4]

The lives of Richard Richards and Douglas Mawson, before, during and after their Antarctic adventures are strikingly similar. These two men stand side by side in any examination of brave and heroic deeds by Australians in the Antarctic. Richards and Mawson were both young scientists. Richards was a junior member who evolved into a leader. Mawson was the leader of his expedition. When placed in life threatening situations both men demonstrated an extraordinary will to live. Richards helped rescue his companions, although Mawson's companions lost their lives. Richards was awarded a medal. Mawson became famous.

It is unarguable that Douglas Mawson remains Australia's greatest Antarctic explorer, but Richards life-saving heroics place him in a very special place in the annals of the history of the Antarctic from 100 years ago.

However, there is little public knowledge about Richards' life and his life saving heroics. He has never received the recognition this author believes he is due.

Richards at Cape Evans.

***

[3] From *South: Shackleton's Endurance Expedition,* by Ernest Shackleton.

[4]   E., Maddison, B. & Norris, K. (2019). Beyond the Heroic Stereotype: Sidney Jeffryes and the Mythologising of Australian Antarctic History. Australian Humanities Review, (64), 1-23.T

Postscript

Richard Richards

In 1923 Richards was awarded the Albert Medal in bronze, for saving life on land. (This medal has now been replaced by the George Cross.) In his later years Richards could never quite figure out why they were awarded the medal as, in his words:

> "...we were only saving our own lives, and we could scarcely do that and leave the others behind."

In the Antarctic, *Richards Inlet* at 83°20'S 168°30'E, is a large ice-filled inlet at the mouth of Lennox-King Glacier, at the opening to the Ross Ice Shelf just southeast of Lewis Ridge. It is the only Antarctic landmark dedicated to the boy from Long Gully.

Richards also received a Polar medal, a medal presented to people who participated in a polar expedition endorsed by a Commonwealth Government. (It was awarded to most members of Shackleton's 1914–1917 expedition.)

Richards returned to the Ballarat School of Mines to lecture in Mathematics and Physics and did this until 1946. He was then appointed Principal of the Ballarat School of Mines. In 1958 he retired, and the Richard W. Richards Medal was instituted by the School. It is awarded annually to the final year student who was considered to have achieved the most outstanding academic performance in Engineering or Science.

Richards outlived all other members of Shackleton's 1914-1917 Imperial Trans-Antarctic Expedition, dying at the age of 91 in 1985. He was the last survivor of the so-called 'Heroic Age' of Antarctic exploration.

Harry Ernest Wild

Wild returned to naval duty on HMS Pembroke in 1917, later transferring to HMS Biarritz. He died on 10 March 1918 in the Royal Naval Hospital, Malta, after contracting typhoid.

He was (posthumously) awarded the Albert Medal for his efforts to save the lives of Mackintosh and Spencer-Smith.

Ernest Mills Joyce

Joyce returned to New Zealand in 1917 and he married Beatrice Curtlett from Christchurch. They kept one of the four dogs-Gunnar – who lived with them until the dog died.

Joyce was awarded the Albert Medal for his efforts to save the lives of Mackintosh and Spencer-Smith. In 1929 he published a book: *The South Polar Trail,* his log of The Imperial Trans-Antarctic Expedition. Joyce died in 1940.

Author Note

During the years 2004 to 2013 I visited the Scott Polar Research Institute in Cambridge, the Melbourne Museum, the Canterbury Museum in Christchurch, the James Caird Library at the National Maritime Museum in London, the Royal Geographical Society in London, the Alexander Turnbull Library in Wellington and the Federation University in Victoria (formerly University of Ballarat), and other places, where I pored over diaries and documents of the men of the Ross Sea party, Shackleton's support party on his famous 1914-1917 Imperial Trans-Antarctic Expedition, the expedition where his boat the *Endurance* was crushed in the ice .

My book *Shackleton's Heroes* was published in 2015 after I had completed my research. The book essentially focussed on the gripping tale of six men who struggled to return to safety after putting down a chain of food depots for Shackleton's use, if he had made his Antarctic crossing.

What struck me, during my research and after the book was published, was what a wonderful film this story would make. I felt it could be a classic; a tale of a young heroic Australian and his adventures with five Englishmen – men of such varied backgrounds, education, experience, and personalities – on how they performed together carrying out unbelievably brave and gallant work under harrowing conditions.

So, I started to write a screen play, a film script, built mainly around the Australian Richard Richards, and his adventures with these Englishmen. It was not the hauling of sledges that particularly enthralled me for a possible film, nor the distance they travelled each day, but more the personal relationship between these men, and their attitudes and outlook, particularly at the times when they were close to death.

But, as enamoured as I was with my early attempt at a film script, after an interview with Phillip Adams on Radio National in 2016, where we discussed *Shackleton's Heroes,* and had a private conversation where he mentioned that he had always wanted to produce or direct a film about Shackleton, I decided to write a book first of all. With a smidgeon of luck it may become the basis of a film about Richard Richards, The Boy from Long Gully.

And, low and behold, the wonderful people at Blue Sky Publishing were also captivated by Richards' years in the Antarctic – Diane Evans who originally pitched the book, and then Allison Paterson, Publishing Consultant/Editor and Sharon Evans, PR/Marketing Director.

My thanks to my sister Jessie Jean Walker for the portraits in the book, my late brother Ian Ferguson McOrist for maps and sketches, and to illustrators Joenovan Ksatrya I and Bill Newton for other sketches.

Sources

Institutions visited to obtain source material included the Alexander Turnbull Library, Wellington, New Zealand, the Royal Geographical Society, London, United Kingdom, the Canterbury Museum, Christchurch, New Zealand, the James Caird Library at the National Maritime Museum in Greenwich, London, United Kingdom, the Melbourne Museum, Melbourne, Australia, and the Scott Polar Research Institute, Cambridge, United Kingdom.

The primary sources used were Richards interview with L. Bickel in 1976, Richards interview with P Lathlean in 1976, Richards interview on the Australian Broadcasting Commission 'Verbatim' program broadcast in 2002, Richards interview with P. Law in December 1980, and the field diaries of Victor George Hayward, Ernest Edward Mills Joyce, Aeneas Lionel Acton Mackintosh, Richard Walter Richards, Arnold Patrick Spencer-Smith, Harry Ernest Wild and Irvine Gaze.

Secondary Sources included: 'Shackleton's Heroes' by the author, 'Antarctic Diaries' of D. Mawson, 'Antarctic Historic Huts'. New Zealand Antarctic Heritage Trust booklet, 'Antarctic Padre', A.J.T. Fraser, unpublished, 'Bio of Frank Wild', Thompson, unpublished, Hayward, radio telegram to Ethel Bridson, Hayward, Peter John, Grand-nephew of Victor Hayward, private papers, Joyce letters, Mackintosh letters, 'Medical Report of the Ross Sea Base ITAE, January 1917.' J.L. Cope, Naval Service Record of Ernest Edward Mills Joyce, No: 160823, Naval Service Record of Harry Ernest Wild, No: 181904, 'Old Woodbridgian' school magazine, Woodbridge School, Suffolk, UK, Anne Phillips, Anne, granddaughter of Aeneas Mackintosh. Private papers, and interview, Report of Proceedings of the Aurora Relief Expedition 1916-1917, Richards Agreement with Shackleton, written December 1914, at Sydney, Australia, Richards Agreement with Shackleton, written January 18th, 1916 in Antarctica, Richards letters and lettergrams to Mackintosh, Richards, various letters to historians, A.J.T. Fraser and L.B. Quartermain, Richards papers at the Art & Historical Collection, Federation University (formerly University of Ballarat), 'Scott's last Expedition, The Journals.' Shackleton's letters to Mackintosh, Shackleton letter to his wife Emily, August 17, 1914, *Shackleton's lieutenant: The Nimrod diary of A.L.A. Mackintosh, South* by E.H. Ernest Shackleton. Spencer-Smith letters, 'The Dial', Queens College Magazine, Queens College, Cambridge, UK, 1907, 'The Eagle', Bedford Modern School (BMS Archives). Journal of 1917, *The Heart of the Antarctic Vol 1* by E.H. Shackleton, *The Ross Sea Shore Party* by R.W. Richards, *The South Polar Trail—The Log of the Imperial Trans-Antarctic Expedition* by Ernest Joyce, *Voyage of the Discovery* by R.F. Scott, *To the South Pole* by Roald Amundsen, 'Willesden Chronicle' newspaper, Willesden Green, UK and *With the Aurora in the Antarctic* by J.K. Davis.

Back Cover Material

A little-known survival story from 100 years ago that embodies the will-to-live of Douglas Mawson, the heroics of Ernest Shackleton, the tragedy of Captain Robert Scott and an Aussie hero from Long Gully.

In 1914, Richard Richards abandons his comfortable life as a science teacher in Australia, to join a support party for Ernest Shackleton, in a very unfamiliar place; the Antarctic.

Due to unforeseen circumstances Richards and a number of his companions become stranded in the Antarctic. However, despite his comparative youth, and inexperience in polar conditions, Richards adapts and survives, unlike some of his companions. He becomes more than an integral member of the team; he takes over a leadership role. He demonstrates what humans can do to stay alive, against near-impossible odds.

The Boy from Long Gully provides the reader with a thrilling insight into the mind-blowing and harrowing ordeal of twenty-two-year-old Richards. It is an utterly riveting story, one of the most amazing tales from a bygone era; the so-called Heroic Age in the Antarctic.

Richard Richards is awarded the Albert Medal in 1923, for his heroism and gallantry in saving life in the Antarctic, the only Australian ever to be so honoured.

However, with the Australian public today he is almost unknown. He is an unsung hero, but he ranks alongside Douglas Mawson in any yardstick of famous Australians from the early 1900s 'Heroic Age of Antarctic Exploration'.

www.ingramcontent.com/pod-product-compliance
Lightning Source LLC
Chambersburg PA
CBHW011736220426
43661CB00062B/2871